Divine Inspirations

Keys To Living A Divine Life

Lisa Nicole Bell

iUniverse, Inc.
New York　Bloomington

Divine Inspirations
Keys To Living A Divine Life

Copyright © 2009 Lisa Nicole Bell. All rights reserved.

All rights reserved. No part of this book may be used or reproduced by any means, graphic, electronic, or mechanical, including photocopying, recording, taping or by any information storage retrieval system without the written permission of the publisher except in the case of brief quotations embodied in critical articles and reviews.

iUniverse books may be ordered through booksellers or by contacting:

iUniverse
1663 Liberty Drive
Bloomington, IN 47403
www.iuniverse.com
1-800-Authors (1-800-288-4677)

Because of the dynamic nature of the Internet, any Web addresses or links contained in this book may have changed since publication and may no longer be valid. The views expressed in this work are solely those of the author and do not necessarily reflect the views of the publisher, and the publisher hereby disclaims any responsibility for them.

ISBN: 978-1-4401-1544-8 (sc)
ISBN: 978-1-4401-1545-5 (ebook)

Printed in the United States of America

iUniverse rev. date: 1/14/2009

Dedication

To the most wonderful parents in the world, Vera and George

And to every human being who longs to be, do, and have more according to God's will

Table of Contents

Dedication	v
Acknowledgements	ix
Introduction	xi
Chapter 1: Divine Living Defined	1
Chapter 2: The Source of Divine Inspiration	15
Chapter 3: Creating Divine Inspirations for Yourself	31
Chapter 4: Cultivating a Divine Environment	53
Chapter 5: Enjoying Divine Relationships	67
Chapter 6: Sustaining A Divine Life	91
Chapter 7: A Call To Action	105
A Special Invitation	109
Personal Inventory Worksheet	111
About the Author	113

Acknowledgements

All praise and honor belongs to the source of all power and intelligence, my Heavenly Father, who has made me whole and cleansed me of my iniquities. I shall forever be indebted to Him for the inspiration to begin this work, the endurance to continue this work, and the courage to finish this work. I am grateful for His presence and movement in my life and for the countless blessings that have been bestowed upon me.

Mom & Dad, you both are amazing. Thank you for being phenomenal people and wrapping your loving arms around me each time I needed it. Thank you for listening to me ramble, being my sounding board, cheering me on and gently guiding me along my path. I love you both dearly. I hope I've made you proud.

To Tatiana J. – thank you, thank you, thank you. Your encouragement and kind words motivated and inspired me countless times. You are such a wonderful friend and accountability partner. Your faith in me kept me going on many days. I only hope I can be as good to you as you are to me. Continue to let your light shine. I love you.

To Valorie Burton, Terrie Williams, and Nelson Davis – thank you for encouraging a budding entrepreneur. Your words to me have inspired me and helped push me to new heights.

Randall, thank you for helping me make it through the publishing process alive! You are quite patient and kind, and I appreciate you.

A huge thank you goes out to those who encouraged me and cheered me on throughout this process: my blog readers, my friends, my associates and my fans. Thank you for your support and loyalty.

A big thank you goes out to every person who's ever bad-mouthed me, persecuted me, shorted me, wronged me, cheated me, lied to me and hated me. You have strengthened me beyond compare, and your contributions to my life have made me a resilient woman. Without going through the fire, I would not be what I am today – pure gold. In order to experience the abundant joy I have, I had to endure some pain.

Finally, I want to thank everyone who has purchased this book. I hope your hearts and minds are blessed by this work. May your days be blessed and your troubles be few. God bless you.

Introduction

The chief cause of failure and unhappiness is trading what you want most for what you want now. – Zig Ziglar

This book was written with achievement, happiness, and abundance in mind. It was written to assist you in becoming the very best version of you that is available. Many of us are living in places of untapped and unrealized potential. It's time to explore the gold mines that lie inside of us all and to begin employing the talents, skills, and knowledge at our fingertips. Everything you need in order to be happy, healthy, and fulfilled is within your reach at this very moment. Do you believe that? If not, you should continue reading. This book will give you insights on what it means to live a divinely inspired life – to live each day in complete realization of God's gifts of life, love, and well-being. Joy and peace are yours for the taking today! So, let us begin on this journey of fashioning a new life – a divine life.

This book was written to inspire, motivate, and uplift people who wish to be, have, and do MORE. I waffled with having the word "abundance" in the title of this book because one of the main ideas is that a person of God can and should enjoy abundance in life. Abundance means different things to different people, but the principle remains the same. A person of God should be one who is happy, fulfilled, self-actualized, and wealthy. Don't confuse wealth with greed or excess. Abundance is used in the Bible, and we're often reminded that God wants to pour out blessings on us that we don't even have the room to accommodate. That's some kind of blessing, don't you think?

Part of the pursuit of this abundance and this inspired lifestyle requires a decision and a commitment to live purposefully. Many people live their lives on accident instead of living them on purpose. Allowing our circumstances to determine what we can and cannot do is living on accident. Believing that we can't achieve our goals because of lack and limitation is living on accident. Allowing whatever will be to be is living on accident. While there will be situations in our lives that will require us to surrender to what is so, we must be vigilant in our purposeful living lest we become fatalists.

We control our destinies! YOU control YOUR destiny. Did you get that? That's something to be excited about. Think about all of the things you've ever dreamed of doing and the things you want to accomplish during your lifetime…now imagine yourself achieving those things and more. How does that feel? Pretty amazing, right? What would it mean to you and those around you if you brought those things to pass with God's help? Well, I'm here to tell you that not only is it possible, but YOU have every resource you need to set about achieving your goals and dreams. Abundance and divine living can be yours. Happiness can be yours. Your dreams can come true. — Miss Independent

It all begins with a choice. So, before we embark on this divine journey together, I want you to make a decision. Decide what's important to you. Decide how you want your life to look. Decide who you want to be. Decide what you want to have. Think about what makes you truly happy. Now, make a decision. Do you want those things? Are you ready to pursue those things and attain them? Are you ready for God to pour out the blessing you don't have room to receive? Are you ready for something different?

If your decision is yes, I encourage you to get a notebook for journaling and a Bible. Keep your notebook, your Bible, and this book together for quick and easy references. I'm going to periodically point you to scriptures to validate my points and help connect the spiritual aspects of abundant living. Revelations of various sorts may come to you as you move through this book, and I want you to keep track of those things. Although many of the ideas sound nice and look good on paper, they will only come alive for you when you begin to apply them to your life immediately.

Beyond your journal and Bible, I want you to bring an open-mind and a positive attitude to the book. No matter how difficult things have been for you, YOU have the power to turn things around. No matter how great things have been for you, YOU have the power to capitalize on your potential and your resources.

If you haven't made a decision to pursue excellence yet, keep reading. You just may find your divine inspiration in these pages.

Chapter 1: Divine Living Defined

The divine life is one that retains its significance long after you are no longer present. —Lisa Nicole Bell

Divine living is comprehensive.

A divinely inspired life is not one that happens on accident. Divine living requires that we wake up each morning with the resolve to give ourselves and those we love our very best. The key to the all-encompassing divine life is transformation. Each morning, when you arise, what do you say to yourself? Do you sigh and dread the coming day or do you wake up excited about the possibilities the day will bring? If it's the former, it's time to make some changes! This may be a sign that something in your life is not working or that something is missing. Either way, you must commit to a life that is inspired by God and filled with the things you love the most.

Infusing your environment with peace, love, happiness, and purpose should be done all around. Often times, we're tempted to give love and devotion to friends but not our spouses. Sometimes we give so much energy to our careers and church work that we neglect the people in our lives who love and appreciate us. We have to commit to systematically transforming our lives into a series of wonderful experiences rather than a string of mediocre days. Divine living permeates all that we do because it's a genuine internal change rather than a temporary, superficial adjustment. With a light inside of us, we can't help but shine our light on those around us.

In God's Word, we are instructed to be transformed by the renewing of our minds. Transformation can be pivotal in our lives if we will allow ourselves to be molded by the beauty of our experiences. Transformation is a universal constant that affects our lives from the moment we are born until we leave this earth. The only guarantee we have in life is that things will always change. At the root of all growth, we find change.

Occasionally, change and the circumstances leading up to it are a source of extraordinary joy, but more often than not they provoke feelings of discomfort, fear, or pain. It is natural for us to be uncertain or concerned about change. However, if we begin to see change as a gentle nudge from God to move us in the right direction, we can appreciate the gift of changes and varied experiences. There are many changes that will happen suddenly and unexpectedly, but we must remember that our God has everything under control. He is not a God of whim or impulse, and the things that appear to be in chaos around us are often in a state of perfect motion according to God's plan. At the heart of every transformation, no matter how chaotic, there is purpose.

Our response to our circumstances is responsible for our happiness or lack thereof. Matthew 6:25-33 tells us not to worry because none of us can add a single hour to our lives by worrying. Besides, God knows exactly what we need and when we need it. When we no longer resist change and instead regard it as an opportunity to grow, we find that we are far from helpless in the face of it. Our commitment to divine living must not waiver, even in the face of adversity and hardship.

God can give us the discernment and wisdom to walk circumspectly and live purposefully. God is not stingy with His wisdom; James 1:5 tell us that He gives to all who ask. In order to claim the wisdom God can bestow upon us, we must learn to fully trust Him and accept the changes taking place all around us.

To begin your transformation and to make change work in your favor, look constructively at supposed problems and circumstances and ask yourself how you can benefit from what has taken place. As threatening as change can seem, it is often a sign that something new and wonderful is waiting for you. I often say that when we think our lives are over, they've usually just begun. If you reconsider your plans and goals in the days or weeks following a major change, you will discover that you are incredibly resilient and that your changes come with many open doors. Upon closing a door, God always opens another, but we often miss the blessings of our changes because we're too busy fretting over the closed door. Optimism, enthusiasm, and flexibility are wonderful assets to draw on amidst change, as there is nothing to be gained by dwelling on what might have been. Change can hurt in the short term, but if you are willing to find the silver lining on the cloud of doubt, its lasting impact will nearly always be physically, spiritually, and intellectually transformative.

In keeping with seeing the beauty of the change in our lives, we should be sure to let go of the past. Psychologists have long asserted that unhealthy fixations on the past or what could have been are detrimental to our mental and emotional health. When we learn to develop flexible personalities, we are better able to adapt to change and respect God's hand at work in our lives.

Divine living is excellent.

Divine living isn't about perfection. The struggle for perfection is something that we've all wrestled with at one time or another. We all hold ideals in our minds of how we wish things would be or how things could be. What we must remember is that our flaws, shortcomings, and imperfections are what make us perfect after all. 2 Corinthians 12:9 says that our weakness is made perfect in His strength. Our weaknesses serve many purposes in our lives. They teach us to value and nurture relationships. When we come to a point of realizing that we need the people God has placed in our lives, we can embrace the gifts of love people choose to give us and give the same love in return. Our weaknesses also keep us grounded. Imagine how life would be if you never made another mistake. Over time, your ego would inevitably inflate to an inordinate size. With that in mind, we can embrace our weaknesses and imperfections and keep them in perspective.

While perfection is a moving target, excellence is not. As people of God, we should be constantly striving to be excellent according to our calling as noted in 1 Peter 2:9. This means that we should seek excellence in all areas of our lives. On our jobs, we should be a light to our co-workers, and God's presence should be evident in the way we conduct ourselves. In the church, we should be busy working for the Lord and serving those around us. In our homes, we should be busy nurturing our spouses and training up our children. With our friends, we should be demonstrating God's love. In all that we do, God should radiate through us in speech and in action.

In keeping with releasing the need for perfection, we must come to a place of healthy acceptance of our shortcomings and regrets. Carrying around shattered dreams and dashed hopes is no way to live! Regret, if not checked, will eat you alive. Regret doesn't get as much publicity as guilt or depression, but regret is lethal in its own right. We have to make it a point to not waste valuable time regretting things...decisions, people, relationships, situations, circumstances. What's done is done, and as I mentioned earlier, Matthew 6 tells us that none of us can add an hour to our lives by worrying. The passage assures us that God is fully aware of what we need and has not made a mistake. When we spend time agonizing over the past, we waste energy, and our spirits are stifled as a result of allowing this kind of negativity to seep into our minds. The bottom line of of a mistake is that there's nothing that can be done about it after the fact. When we are wrong, we should ask for forgiveness from others and God, and move on. When circumstances prevent achievement, what can you do? Rather than bathe in self-pity, the lesson in the disappointment has to be taken and added to your arsenal of experiences. Regret does not serve ambition, excellence, hope, or progress so it's better left locked up and thrown away. Making peace with poor decisions and transgressions of the past is a gateway to fearlessly making decisions and enjoying freedom from the bondage of regret. God intended for us to live without the weight of the past.

Divine living is a full-time job ordained by God.

Many Christians are guilty of part-time work. We have failed to realize that our spirituality is a 24 hour commitment. It is not a way to live on Sunday or when it's convenient. Our relationship with God should directly influence our value systems which should in turn dictate where we go, what we do, and how we live. We must keep our callings at the front of our minds. Too many of us are holy, saved, and sanctified on Sunday complete with a choir robe and a Bible to match, but when Monday morning rolls around, we're calling our co-workers everything but a child of God and by the time Saturday arrives, we're ready to put on the best threads we can find to go out to some den of iniquity and do things we know we shouldn't be doing.

It's time to ask yourself when it will stop. When will you be sold out for God? When will God's opinion of you matter more than that of your friends and family? When will God be the judge and jury of your life instead of you and the voices of your head? God has so much in store for us that remains untapped because our relationship with Him is not where it should be. We cannot be mad at God for not blessing our mess.

Allow me to share part of my story. I've always considered myself a decent Christian. I was raised in the church, and I was active through my childhood and into high school. When I left home to move to California, I started questioning everything about my life. Up until that point, my religion and much of what I believed about life and how it should be lived had been handed to me. It was never forced on me, but my parents had done what most good parents do: they provided me with guidance and instruction while I lived in their household. When I moved out, I started questioning those things. I spent a lot of time alone discovering who I really was as a person and what type of life I wanted to craft for myself. I spent time praying, reading my Bible, fasting, and writing. I wanted to be closer to God; I wanted to understand my purpose and how I fit into His plan. After many changes and many tears, I realized that I didn't agree with much of what I had been taught as a child in a southern Baptist church. Much of the doctrine was, in my opinion, pompous and ungrounded, and I sought out other aspects of religion and spirituality in order to figure out what God had for me. Eventually, I realized and accepted the fact that I simply am not a religious person and probably never will be. By nature, I'm not the person who will snub others for not wearing the right outfit on the right Sunday nor will I pretend to catch the Spirit when I am not moved. I am, however, very spiritual. I am a firm believer in God's anointing on my spirit and his endowment of various talents and gifts. I believe in maintaining an intimate relationship with God. Whether I choose to worship on Saturday or Sunday, whether I choose to wear pants or dresses, whether I can speak in tongues or not - I'm still a child of God, and He loves me in spite of me. I believe that He sends people and situations into our lives for a reason, always a spiritual one, to teach us lessons and help us grow as people. I believe that God wants abundance and prosperity for me and His people, and I know that He is faithful in all things. The major lesson that I learned was that being a woman of God - not a part-time Christian, not a Christian when it's convenient - but a real woman of God, requires commitment, dedication, awareness, and much prayer. Slowly but surely, I saw myself becoming a woman after God's heart, and through much soul searching and prayer, He has revealed Himself to me in various aspects of my life.

This book is a manifestation of one of those revelations. That doesn't mean I've never fallen short or that I'm remotely close to perfection, but it does mean that I'm forgiven, and that I'm growing every day. I have to remind myself that in my speech, my lifestyle, and my actions, others should see God...not a "holy roller", not a "Jesus freak" but a woman who is upright and striving for excellence and Godliness in her existence. I want to be an inspiration to those around me, and from my observations, that happens when I allow God to use me as His vessel. With God at the helm of our lives, we must be more aware of the details, the small things that are easily overlooked that make the difference. There should never be a question about whether God is present and real in our lives. Matthew 7:16 tells us that we can recognize other believers by their fruit. What kind of fruit are you producing? Is it bitter or sweet? As we commit to complete service to God, we can be sure that the fruit we produce is of the Spirit and can be easily recognized by others.

Divine living is largely centered on relationships.

Relationships are an essential part of our lives. You may have heard the saying, "No man is an island." It's true that none of us can operate independently of other people so it's important that you know how to effectively interact with others and how to develop healthy relationships. Study after study has shown that those who are connected with others and regularly commune with others are healthier and live longer than those who don't. Healthy relationships are essential to our well-being as humans. Our society places tremendous emphasis on individuality and self-efficiency, but the truth of the matter is that we all crave human interaction. God created us for each other. If this were not so, He would have left Adam alone in the Garden of Eden with the animals. We are hard wired to talk, laugh, play, and love one another. With this understanding, divine living places tremendous emphasis on the creation and cultivation of healthy relationships. This can include people as close as our spouses and as distant as total strangers. Ultimately, we are all connected, and we are all God's creation. It's easy for us to go about our days thinking we are alone with our thoughts, quirks, fears, worries, and hopes. We fail to realize that others around us experience the same human emotions that we do.

Cultivating divine relationships requires that we learn to communicate effectively, practice empathy, and become safer people. Communication is the bridge over the waters of disagreement that would prove to tear us away from those who care about us. Empathy is the act of putting oneself in the shoes of another for the sake of appreciating that person's feelings. When we practice empathy, we put ourselves in a position to give the love others need and gain much in the process. Becoming safer people involves being courageous enough to live out our truths every day. It means being honest with our loved ones and learning to accept them as they are and relinquish our needs to be right or to mold them into who we believe they should be.

While our relationships are certainly not limited to those of a romantic nature, an important place to practice divine living is in our romantic relationships. At some point, you may decide to enter into a romantic relationship with someone. Perhaps you already have. Either way, it's important that we develop tools for assessing how fit a person is for us and vice versa since our love interests are typically closer to us than others. This knowledge, if applied, will help you avoid some heartache and disappointment or lighten the burden of a broken relationship.

Before getting involved with a person, ask yourself what you want. Don't run down a list of clichés; ask yourself what is really important to you in *your* life and in your relationships. Knowing your priorities makes choosing a partner much easier. People may come into your life who seem great on paper but may not necessarily be right for you. The best way to navigate those fuzzy lines is to know exactly who you are, what you stand for, and what you want out of life. If your potential mate's values don't align with your own, you'll want to address those differences to avoid future conflict. This same principle applies to friends and associates. I always tell people to ask the tough questions now so that you can have peace later.

We all have our deal breakers, and we all have things we "prefer" but could live without if necessary. Spend some time thinking about what your deal breakers are. Is it smoking? Is it a certain number of children? Is it religion? Is it support in your career? There are no right or wrong answers. As a human being, you're entitled to your thoughts, opinions, and feelings. Own yourself and your belief system and allow it to be your guide in choosing who to let in to your world. Seek God's opinion on the matter, and allow the Holy Spirit to gently guide you towards the people who belong in your life. This topic is so important to me that I wrote an entire stage play entitled *Deal Breakers*. In the play, we observed friends, associates, and lovers interacting with each other and creating spoken and unspoken agreements. Ultimately, the story taught that deal breakers exist for us whether we acknowledge them or not.

Remember that even though you may not be looking for a spouse at this point in your life, it's important that you get into the habit of discerning an excellent person from a mediocre person and that you get used to being treated well. We teach others how to treat us. If you spend time meditating, doing things you enjoy, eating well, and so forth, others will see how well you treat yourself and assume that they must treat you just as well if they are to be allowed to remain in your life. Setting a standard for yourself in dating and socializing and adhering to it will earn you the respect of yourself and others. Without loving yourself, you can't love others! If you command excellence, love, positive energy, and respect, you'll receive it. If you accept anything less, you'll receive less.

Once you set a standard, stick to it! No matter how cute, rich, flashy, popular, accomplished or sought after a person is, stick to what *you* know is right. Your intuition and common sense have been given to you as gifts to guide you on your path through life. When you ignore that little voice or that nagging feeling, you are essentially telling God and yourself that you've got it under control. Don't ignore your built-in protection mechanisms! It's never a good idea to compromise who you are or what you believe in for another person. You'll be forced to continue to compromise yourself throughout the course of the relationship, and at some point, you'll probably fold under the pressure to be something or someone you're not. Compromising on issues is one thing; that's a part of any friendship or marriage, but compromising yourself will lead to confusion, pain, and heartache.

So, think deeply about who you are at your core and what you want in your life. Think about the ideal mate; think about the qualities that are most important to you. Pray for revelation of God's purpose and will for you. Ask yourself how you like to be treated and what kinds of things enhance your life. These will be the critical things to look for in your assessments.

Finally, know that having standards and being a truthful, self-actualized person isn't easy. You may spend a little more time searching than you anticipated, but having authentic love with a person who respects and cherishes you will be well worth the wait. In the mean time, prepare yourself to receive the gift of love and healthy acceptance that will be yours.

Divine living requires an understanding of personal purpose.

Knowing your purpose is an important part of knowing who you are and going after the things that are destined to be yours. Purpose is the seed of inspiration and the motivation to persevere through hardships and adversities. Understanding why you were put here gives you something to hope for, something to do, and something to love. All of these things are essential to leading a fulfilling life.

Take a moment to think about the meaning of life. Do you know why you were created? Do you know what the purpose of your life is? It's not the end of the world if you don't because you can begin discovering those things right away. Know that discovering and understanding your purpose is essential to your existence. Purpose acts as a motivator and a guide for your life by helping you to refocus when you're distracted and guiding you towards your goals when you're uncertain about what your next move should be.

Divine Inspirations

You are special; no one else will ever be like you. Therefore, you serve a special purpose on this earth. God has set a certain task aside just for you because He knows that you can complete this task like no one else can. To attempt to be like someone else is to insult God's handiwork. He did not make any mistakes on you! We often think that God must have been too busy to give us a total package, but He is flawless in His creation and execution. We are created in His image, and we are fearfully and wonderfully made!

Your purpose can provide you with many things you need to live the life of your dreams. Do you dream of being a doctor? A model? A teacher? Whatever it is, you can take your dreams a step further by adding purposeful meaning to them. In addition to contributing to a feeling of happiness and well-being, purpose can provide you with a road map for where to go, what to do, and how to do it. When you feel lost or discouraged, your purpose can gently lead you back to safety. We often find ourselves getting caught up in the routines of our lives. Purposeful lives are those that are not simply "filled up"; purposeful lives are those that are filled with meaning. You may have noticed that people who are successful seem to get so much more done than average people. However, we are all afforded 24 hours in every day. So how do successful people manage to accomplish so much more than everyone else? The answer is purpose.

Too many people are going about their daily routines living lives that are the result of circumstances instead of choosing to live the lives they desire. Ask yourself some important questions. What are my dreams? What do I really want to do? If I could wake up tomorrow and do anything I wanted, what would it be? What do I see myself doing in 5 years? 10 years? On my death bed, what will I want to have accomplished? What do I want to be able to say about my life as I reflect on it? Assess the possibility of your dreams and ambitions. Nothing is impossible. God happens to specialize in the impossible. You only need faith, passion and perseverance in order to bring your desires to fruition.

If you're unsure of what your purpose is, don't panic. I'm here to help you discover that purpose and to live in it each and every day from this day forward. You have time to freely pursue the things that inspire you and to change your mind, if you desire. Imagine the possibilities of things you can accomplish in your lifetime. No dream is too big! If you believe it, you can definitely achieve it. That extends to all of your goals and dreams, both big and small. If you have a dream, pursue it! Ask God what His will is for you, and allow your conversations with Him to be a guide for your endeavors. He will guide you to the exact place you should be and give you the tools to do everything He has for you. It is natural to feel nervous or fearful in the face of a new adventure, but remember that God will give you everything you need to become the best person you can be.

Along the way, you'll need the assistance of various people, places, and things. Don't allow fear to prevent you from boldly going after the things you want. The Bible says, "According to your faith, shall it be done unto you." Therefore, you have to believe God will give you everything you need to complete the task He's given you to fulfill your purpose. Faith is the key that unlocks the door to the abundance that should be in our lives.

So the question is: how do we discover our purpose? There are several ways to go about it. Some people use discovering purpose and discovering self interchangeably. The truth is that we will always be who we are. There's no need to find ourselves. Instead, we should be on a quest to find our purpose as God has ordained it. It is in His perfect will that we find peace, success, happiness, and the desires of our hearts. As George Bernard Shaw so eloquently put it, "Life is not about finding yourself. Life is about creating yourself."

One important method for discovering your purpose is to spend some time alone thinking about what it is you want out of life and what you would like to achieve. You probably spend a considerable amount of time with your friends, family members, church members, and classmates. Over time, these people and their opinions influence your own thought patterns and opinions. It's easy to go along with the crowd since there is strength in numbers. Also, you probably assume that you'll have the support of those nearest to you if you do as they wish. However, it is extremely important that you develop your own identity, your own opinions, and your own dreams. This may call for some quiet time alone with yourself and God, but the things you will discover will be well worth the investment of time. Begin by spending 15-30 minutes a day pondering your greater purpose in life. Think outside of your current parameters. Think about your future. What kinds of things do you envision yourself doing? What kind of changes would you like to see in the world around you? In 20 years, how would you like for your life to look? What would you attempt to do if you knew you could not fail?

Spend some time journaling about these things. Begin writing down ideas for the types of things you'd like to do. You'd be surprised how many things can earn income for you if you spend time planning and organizing your resources. Dream big! Don't skip over any hunch or idea. Allow your mind to go wild with imaginative and inspired thought. After you're done journaling, take a look at what you've written. Are the things you see related in any way? Perhaps you've discovered a desire to work in the arts or maybe you're realizing that many of your dreams involve helping people. Whatever it is, you may be able to focus on one of your goals and expand it into a career choice or a passion project. This type of exercise may reveal things you hadn't considered before.

Another tool for discovering purpose is something I call self-inventory. In the back of this book, there is a self-inventory form that will give you an outline for taking inventory on yourself. Taking inventory gives you an opportunity to see yourself on paper. Doing so will allow you to objectively assess your talents and abilities. With knowledge of where you excel, you can begin applying those talents and abilities in areas where they can be most effective.

So, know your purpose before you do anything else as purpose is essential to everything you do. Your daily actions will require that your purpose be clear and present for you every day of your life. This awareness will propel you toward success!

In moving towards a life of divine inspiration, we have to examine what is required to live a life of divine inspiration. There are many traits that God has called His people to have, but we will concentrate on a few for our purposes. We'll discuss the importance of developing a healthy, active relationship with yourself, God and others, and we'll examine ways to create a divine environment. At the end of this book, you'll have practical insights on how to live a life inspired by God and designed by you.

- Things I am proud of
  graduation certificate
    my name Reena kaushal.
    graduating from the
    coaching Intensive
    training program.

  → HR

Chapter 2: The Source of Divine Inspiration

God enters by a private door into each individual.
– Ralph Waldo Emerson

The source of divine inspiration can be summed up in one word: GOD. Not the universe, not the earth, not our "inner selves", just God. He alone has the power to elevate us to a higher place of consciousness and grant us every resource we need to succeed in this life. God has also given us each other and our relationships as a source of divine inspiration.

You may have heard older people say, "Keep God first in your life." There's a reason that wise people so often share this nugget of knowledge. They know something about life. They understand that life is an ongoing oscillation of joy and pain, and that even the best lives are laced with trials and tribulations. More importantly, these people understand that there can be no joy without God. He alone can heal our areas of brokenness and grant us the peace that passes all understanding.

In order to tap into divine inspiration, we must first be in communion with God. If you've never felt His presence in your life, you don't know what you're missing! Experiencing God's supernatural touch in life is truly life-transforming. Communion with God can be attained many ways: prayer, meditation, writing, reading the Bible, and fellowship. God has made Himself available in every facet of our lives so that there would be no shortage of opportunities for us to experience His love and the fullness of His plan for our lives. Let's take a closer look at some of the aforementioned paths to communion with God.

Prayer is the most important action we can take in harvesting divine inspiration on a daily basis. God has given us a wonderful vehicle for communicating with Him. It costs us nothing, and it requires little effort on our parts to set aside time to speak candidly with God.

Divine Inspirations

Something supernatural and transformative happens when we spend time talking with God and revealing our concerns, praise, and desires to Him. We can be free to tell Him about everything. A line from a popular song reminds us that we can carry everything to God in prayer. This is so true! There is no reason for us to walk around burdened and emotionally constipated when we have such a wonderful confidant and friend in Christ. He is there to offer up whatever we need. No other entity can give us the comprehensive provisions that God can when we bare our souls to Him in prayer.

When that co-worker has said or done something to upset you, taking a moment to meditate can keep you from flying off the handle and saying something you'll regret. When that church member does something we don't like, meditating can give us time to really consider how God would advise us to handle the situation. When a spouse does something to irritate us, we can step away from the situation to gain some perspective and avoid a potentially bad situation.

Meditating is something rarely done in today's busy society. With so many of us working and tending to responsibilities, it's easy to get caught up in our hectic schedules. Nevertheless, pausing for a moment to bask in the glow of God's love and spend a quiet moment with Him can create more intimacy. The word intimacy is often used to describe an experience shared between a man and a woman, but have you ever paused to consider being intimate with God? What if you were at a place where you could share the deepest, darkest parts of yourself with God? He wants to know you that way! He's so gentle and loving that He never forces Himself upon us. He waits patiently for us to invite Him to the good, bad, and ugly parts of ourselves. Meditating on Him and His Word can create an environment for us to grow more intimate with Him.

Ironically, when we get busy, the first thing that tends to get cut back is our quiet time. We have less time and more on our agendas, so it makes sense that this happens, but in the end, it doesn't really help us. Most of us know from experience that we function much better when we give ourselves time each day to sit in silence. Research has revealed that those who afford themselves quiet time daily are healthier, happier, and more productive than those who don't. The more we have to do, the more we need that solitary, quiet time for the day ahead. Therefore, while it may sound counterintuitive, it is during busy times that we most need to spend more time in meditation rather than less. By being quiet and listening to what God has to say to us, we will be given what we need to get through our day.

Meditating for just 10 minutes each day can make a big difference, as can the addition of short meditations into our daily schedules. Carving out a few extra minutes each day can have huge payoffs. The key is convincing ourselves that spending that time in meditation is the best choice. If God has given us 24 hours in every day to achieve all that we wish, surely we can carve out time to sit in stillness with Him. We often make tradeoffs of one activity for another due to time constraints. Instead of meditating, we could be doing the laundry or getting more work done so it's important that we first come to value the importance of meditation in the context of all the other things competing for attention in our lives. The only way we'll know whether it works to meditate more when we are busy is to try it. We can start the meditation journey by creating more time in the morning, either by getting up earlier or by showering the night before and using the extra time for meditation. We can also add short meditation breaks into our schedule, from five minutes before or after lunch to a meditation at night before we go to sleep. When we come from a place of centered calm, we are more effective in handling our busy schedules and more able to keep our lives in perspective. If more time in meditation means less time feeling anxious, stressed, and overwhelmed, then it's certainly worth the extra time. God's voice is a gentle and quiet one. The voice of the Holy Spirit will never go into overdrive to yell over all the chaos in our lives. If we truly want the gifts that God wants to give us, we must be willing to pause long enough to hear His voice and heed His instruction. I enjoy spending quiet time with God first thing in the morning. There's something about being awakened and realizing that God has afforded me another day that makes me want to enjoy the stillness of the morning and be alone in His presence.

Writing is another tool for developing ourselves spiritually and growing closer to God. Journaling can provide us with an outlet for the energy inside of us. On any given day, we experience a wide range of emotions and experiences. Writing gives us an opportunity to put our experiences into perspective by taking a moment to reflect on what has happened and to articulate our thoughts and feelings. After a while, we can flip back through the pages to see various transitions in our lives. Hindsight is often 20/20, and when we reflect, we can see that things that once seemed like a big deal were not quite as pressing as they seemed or vice versa. Not only does writing put things in perspective, it can be an opportunity for us to communicate our written thoughts and intentions to God. The written word has a special power to it. Seeing our thoughts, ideas, and feelings on paper can inspire, motivate, and comfort us. Use that power to your advantage. A divine element of our lives can be unleashed when we put the pen to the pad.

Perhaps one of the best ways to connect with God and hear His voice is through reading His Word. God was gracious enough to give us the Bible in all of its infinite wisdom. The Bible is full of valuable information for us to use in the navigation of our lives. Not only can we read exciting and interesting stories, we can gain wisdom and insight for our daily lives. We can find practical knowledge for interpersonal relationships, personal affairs, and careers. God can use the Bible to gently speak to us and guide us to where He would have us to be. For this reason, it's important that we do not neglect this opportunity to connect with God and hear His voice. If studying the Bible seems daunting or overwhelming, consider using a study guide or Bible companion like Our Daily Bread. These kinds of references can give you assistance in digesting a slice of God's Word each day. A Bible study class is another great way to learn more about God's Word and gain insights on the practical application of its concepts.

The Bible tells us not to forsake fellowship with other believers. We've often heard the saying that there's strength in numbers. This saying is exceptionally true for people of God. As we make our way through the world striving not to conform to the pattern of the world, we often need to seek encouragement and communion with others who understand our struggles and challenges. God uses people to minister to us, encourage us, and keep us on the proper path toward fulfilling our purposes as Christians.

You may know people or perhaps you are a person who says, "I love God, but I hate church! They're just a bunch of hypocrites." Oftentimes, Christians feel alienated in church by religious dogma, rigid traditions, and judgment. Although God has not ordained these activities for church, they occur. It becomes easy for a new Christian or even an experienced Christian to feel like an outsider being driven away from the church. There is no such thing as a perfect church, nor are there any perfect people. When we consider that the body of Christ is comprised of imperfect people, like ourselves, who are striving to grow closer to God, we may find it easier to appreciate our church-going experience as a journey. God is gracious enough to forgive us for our sins and transgressions in spite of our obstinate and rebellious ways. His patience knows no end. With such a great example of love, we must remember to be patient and graceful with those around us. God has not called us to be hostile, judgmental, or abrasive with one another. Finding the church that is right for us may require some trial and error, but we must remember that fellowship with God's people is essential to our growth as spiritual beings.

Once we've discovered the source of divine inspiration, we should not keep it to ourselves! We should eagerly share the good news with those around us. Jesus came that we might have life and have it more abundantly. As such, we should make it our business to spread the word about God's love. There are many ways we can go about sharing God's Word and His message. When we think of witnessing to others, Bible-thumping, overbearing preaching comes to mind. However, God has not called us to force our beliefs on others or to ridicule those who are not as far along in their walk with Him. Instead, we can graciously find ways to communicate the message.

One of those ways is through action. As I mentioned earlier, the Bible tells us that by their fruit, we shall know them. If a stranger was to look at your fruit, would he recognize you as a child of God? If not, you may need to reconsider the things you say and do. If God is truly living inside of us, He should show up outside of us. Our actions should be an indication that we are a people set apart from the world. My pastor once said that our horizontal relationships are indicative of our vertical relationships. That's certainly food for thought. The state of our relationship with God will reveal itself in how we relate to other people. As Christians, we are to dismiss our worldly desires and submit our will to that of God. Have you done that? If not, there's no better time than the present. Getting our own spiritual homes in order gives us the courage and tools we need to bring others into the Christian flock.

Our speech is just as important as our actions. The tongue has the power of life and death in it according to Proverbs 18:21. That is very powerful! With such tremendous power, it is only right that we are admonished about the power of the tongue in the Bible. In today's modern society, many of us have gotten comfortable and have left our tongues unguarded. We allow all kinds of inappropriate and ungodly talk to flood our speech with no thought for God's opinion. We must remember that Godly living is a full time job. Just because our worldly friends let profanity and vulgarity frequent their speech does not mean we should be overcome by the same tendencies. I've heard all kinds of justifications for using profanity, but I always end the discussion by asking this question: If Jesus were sitting or standing next to you as you spoke each day, would you choose the same words? It's easy to make efforts to rationalize our behavior when the consequences are not immediate. The Bible tells us often to guard our speech and to be careful about what we say. We are called to produce fresh, clean water, and as such, the salt water of negativity and profanity should not also be coming from our springs. Our words should build up and bless rather than tear down and curse.

So we've talked about the importance of being in communion with God and sharing God with others. Now let's examine the other aspects of our lives that have been given to us as gifts and sources of divine inspiration. Our relationships are the second source of divine inspiration. God designed us to enjoy time and interaction with other human beings. We see this as early as creation times when God created Eve to be a companion to Adam. God quickly realized that the animals He had created would be insufficient company for Adam. So, he created Eve to be a helpmeet for Adam. Likewise, God sends people to us to serve a range of purposes. The people in our lives can be encouragers, lovers, friends, listeners, supporters, motivators, and teachers among other things. In all of His love for us, God sends us who we need when we need them. This is why building and maintaining healthy relationships is so important. Second to communication, interpersonal relationship skills are one of the most important traits we can develop in ourselves.

The importance of communication in relationships has almost become cliché. We often hear communication referenced as the most important aspect of a relationship. I'd like to propose that *honest, healthy* communication is the most important aspect of a relationship. In an uncomfortable situation, lying is easier than telling the truth yet the lie is still a form of communication. One of the best ways we can show a person that we care about him/her is by telling the truth. We sometimes tell ourselves that we're doing another person a favor by not telling the truth, but the Bible tells us repeatedly that God is not pleased with lying or people who tell lies. It also speaks of the consequences that will befall those who tell lies. In keeping with this, we should train ourselves to tell the truth in love to those around us, particularly those we love. Furthermore, we have to remember that there is a healthy way to communicate and an unhealthy way to communicate. Yelling, cursing, and saying hurtful things can do irreparable damage to our loved ones. Love is not selfish or hurtful so regardless of how angry or frustrated we become, we have to remember to bridle our tongues and speak clearly and kindly.

When we are connected to the sources of divine inspiration, the fruit of that connection becomes evident in our lives. Kindness is one of the marks of divine inspiration. The importance of kindness in a relationship is often underestimated. The Bible is full of references about the importance of loving actions and kindness. A kind act can soothe a hurting heart or bring a smile to a solemn face. Few people know just how significant the impact of a kind act or word can be. Kindness is an ideal that is easily accessible to all of us. Think for a moment about how you feel when a stranger offers a warm smile to you in passing or when someone lets you over in traffic without a hassle. Even bringing an instance of kindness to mind can put a smile on your face days or weeks later or perhaps even inspire you to share kindness with another. Though it may seem simple to the point of insignificance, kindness is recognized as essential to life in many religions and cultures. The smallest gesture can bring a smile to light the shadow of an unpleasant situation or remove tension from a difficult task, but its effects can echo and extend far beyond the moment. It may be the simplest way to experience and share love and God with humanity. We can make the choice to act from the best place within ourselves at any time, while also recognizing wonderful potential in another with the smallest of acts, nourishing the seed of hope in each soul we encounter.

In a way, kindness acts as the oil that makes the engine of our world move more smoothly and with less friction. We can still get where we are going but the ride is more pleasant, and those around us can share in the divine world that we help to create. We are fortunate that kindness is endless in its supply. It costs nothing and is available to everyone. Whether holding a door open for someone or letting someone go ahead of us in line, donating money or sharing our homes in a crisis, we actively share God's love and kindness with every choice we make. We can be sure that we will receive kindness in return, but giving is its own reward. Kindness expands the light within us and reaches out to touch the light in others as well, giving us all a glimpse of the glow of God's love that has the power to enlighten our world.

We also have to be mindful of the necessity of sustaining our relationships. Many people believe that once a relationship begins, it will continue without assistance in the way a boulder will continue down a hill once it is pushed. Unfortunately, relationships are more complicated than that. They require that we put time, resources, and energy into the people and things we value the most. There are many virtues that can enhance the state of a relationship, but I'd like to address a few important issues surrounding the formation and maintenance of healthy relationships. Not only is it important that we learn to be completely happy with ourselves before we can truly make another happy, we also have to learn to love selflessly. These things are easier said than done, but they can take a relationship to the next level and enhance our lives. In addition to our relationships with God and others, we must also cultivate healthy relationships with ourselves. The following chapter will offer insights on how to inspire and develop divine inspiration in ourselves.

We attract the energy we put out. This law is as old as time, but the Bible alludes to it by asking how two can walk together unless they be agreed. This is important because in our quest for acceptance, love, and friendship, we often lose sight of some important things. In order to assess the type of people we attract, we should first assess ourselves. If you are attracting people who are needy and draining, stop and ask yourself what there is about you that may be attracting these types of people. If you are attracting people who are demanding and rigid, examine what may be attracting these people into your life. Understand that no one can come into your life and stay there without your permission. Part of divine living is living on purpose and that includes our friendships and relationships. As well-adjusted Christian adults, we should be taking the time to evaluate all of the relationships around us. This can include our relationships with those close to us like a spouse or family member or someone not as close like a co-worker or church member. The way we behave in relationships can tell us a lot about what is going on inside of us, and it can help point us to areas where we may need God's help in developing ourselves as Christians.

Many friendships and relationships happen in ways that seem accidental. Perhaps we meet a new friend at Bible study or we run into a college classmate in a store. However these things come about, we must be discerning in who we allow to gain intimate access to our minds and hearts. Proverbs 4:23 tells us to guard our hearts because they are the wellspring of life. We have to be aware of how new people in our lives will affect us. If we go about haphazardly befriending everyone we cross paths with, we will quickly find ourselves in compromising positions because not everyone will share our values, morals, and ethics. Satan can use anyone and anything to throw us off track so we have to keep God's Word and His instruction at the forefront of our minds. When you are considering bringing a new person into your fold, ask yourself some important questions to determine whether you're making the right decision:

Is this person a woman or man of God?

Does this person take his/her Christian walk seriously?

What does this person stand for?

What does this person do with his/her spare time?

What types of things does this person say?

What does this person feed his/her mind with?

Will hanging around this person and growing closer to them draw me closer to or further from God?

If you honestly answer these questions, it will be much easier to determine whether the development of the friendship will be good for your Christian walk or a liability to it. Of course, we all want to witness to those around us and win souls for Christ, but we must be strategic in the way we approach this task. If not, we can quickly find ourselves doing what they do and living the way they live instead of influencing them to do things God's way. Most of the time, we become like the clean hand and the dirty hand. When you rub a clean hand and a dirty hand together, you don't get two clean hands. You get two dirty hands. In our cleanliness, we have to be aware of this and avoid getting dirty with our new friends.

This also applies to those who are already in our lives. These people can be just as much of a threat to our spiritual well-being as new people. Periodically, we need to ask God to reveal the hearts of those around us to us. We want to be able to clearly see who we are dealing with and how we should approach our relationships with those people. The law of association tells us that we become the people we associate with. With such a powerful force at work, we simply cannot afford to spend time with people who are negative, worldly, and emotionally unhealthy.

Most of us come to a point in our lives when we question why we are doing what we are doing, and many of us come to realize that we may be living our lives in an effort to make those around us happy. Moms often experience this as they set about trying to be super woman by being everything to everyone. They take care of the kids, their husbands, their parents and siblings, their co-workers, and everyone else while neglecting their own needs and wants. This realization can dawn when we are in our 20s, our 40s, or even later, depending upon how tight a hold our family of origin has on our psyche. We may feel shocked or depressed by this information, but the revelation always comes at a time when God has equipped us with the mental and emotional resources to do something about it. It may mean that it is time to remove some people from our lives or learn to live for God and ourselves instead of others. Setting healthy boundaries can be the key to our freedom from living up to the expectations of everyone except ourselves.

One of the most common reasons we are so tied into making others happy is that we are not entirely sure of what we want or the direction we should be headed. In life, we all want and need a sense of purpose and direction whether we realize it or not. When we do not have that, we often seek it out wherever it may be found. We must remember that God is not a god of confusion or games. He can and will make His will known to us if we will seek Him. If we truly spend time seeking God and drawing closer to Him, we will be able to discern whether we are in His will. Allowing God's voice to be the compass that guides us will never lead us wrong. We can press forward confidently knowing that God's will never take us where God's grace will not protect us. Looking to outside sources will only leave us frustrated, lost, and confused.

Without doing the internal work to discover what we are best suited for or spending time in prayer to learn what God has for us, we fall back on the expectations of those around us. This is particularly easy to do when we have grown up around a certain group of people and we carry the same relationships into adulthood. If these people do not give us the appropriate space to grow and develop ourselves as individuals, our identity remains attached to these people and their expectations of us. We must consciously make a decision to distance ourselves from people who will not allow us to evolve into the people we want to become. God has not designed us to remain in a single state all of our lives. We must be honored as individuals in our own right, with a will and purpose of our own, to be determined by God's will. With the change of circumstances and environment comes the change of our personalities, our tastes, and our goals. Be aware of people who are so unhappy with themselves that they do whatever they can to put a damper on your happiness. This kind of energy is toxic, and it can get out of hand quickly. We must never lose sight that God is the ultimate authority. He is the source of divine inspiration and as such, we owe our allegiance, our attention, and our submission to Him.

The good news is that the parts of us that have not been adequately nurtured are still there, alive and well, like a seed that has not yet received the sunlight and moisture it needs to open and bloom. It is never too late to ask God for the courage to step out in confidence and faith and be who He has created us to be. This experience of becoming is well worth the uncomfortable moments and hard work that may be required of us to get where we need to be. In the beginning, it's easy to assume that something is wrong because we often feel worse before we feel better when we're making important changes. However, we have to remember that even the most positive of changes can leave us feeling out of our element because we are moving into a new place. The important thing is to press forward, understanding that God is doing a wonderful work inside of us and there is no reason to be afraid or to second guess our decisions that help us live the best lives we possibly can.

Another thing to remember about the events that happen in our lives during a time like this is that every single thing is happening for a specific, God-ordained reason. There are no accidents or coincidences. Every single person who crosses your path is supposed to and every single thing that happens is supposed to happen. When we can accept that everything in our lives is exactly as it should be, we can move forward fearlessly. This same attitude applies to the people who come into our lives who may make us feel uncomfortable. God has a way of bringing us into contact with people who challenge us with their differences. It may be an obvious difference reflected in their outward appearance or an intangible difference like politics or religion. It is with these people and the challenges they present that we learn important lessons about ourselves and how to love God's way. Even in our closest circle of friends and family, we can see vast differences in choices, lifestyle, and preferences. Oftentimes, there is no "right" or "wrong" way of doing something. One way is simply different, and the beauty of these differences is the valuable contribution that we can all make to the world around us. We can choose to resist the differences in others, but we can also choose to learn from them and appreciate that they too have a place in God's plan. Believe it or not, "difficult" people can help us develop and appreciate the divine inspiration God has placed in our lives.

We all claim to want happiness and peace with no struggles, but where would such a life ever get us? We can not truly experience joy without pain. We would not be able to appreciate a beautiful day in the spring without a stormy day in the winter. Our attitudes towards people and situations will determine if we sail over them, confirming our emotional flexibility, or end up frustrated and unhappy. Learning to develop healthy attitudes towards both the good and bad in our lives is perhaps the most important aspect of developing divine inspiration in ourselves. God has given us passage after passage in His Word outlining how we are to handle success and adversity. If we begin applying these precepts, our lives will inevitably take a dramatic shift towards happiness, peace, and love. This is how we learn, grow, and develop ourselves. In a world of competing interests, we have to allow God to define us and give us the inspiration to rise above our struggles. Without challenge, there is nothing to overcome and nothing to learn. Growth is essential to our very livelihood. Without challenges and changes, none of us would be who we are or where we are today. No matter how spiritual we are, we will experience challenges. We will always run into people who are different from us. Rather than give in to the urge to fight or shut down, we can ask God for divine inspiration in order to evolve into better and more meaningful expressions of ourselves.

Before I end this chapter, I'd like to touch on the role of faith in accessing and preserving divine inspiration in our lives. Faith is essential to the survival of the dedicated Christian and the soul who seeks to enjoy divine inspiration. The gift of divine inspiration is like a seed, and faith is the water needed to nourish the seed. Without sufficient water, the seed may suffocate. The Bible places great emphasis on faith. There are many scriptures on faith and the importance of it. Hebrews 11:6 tells us that without faith, it is impossible to please God. I think that drives home the importance of faith. We have to remember that we can only see so much from where we sit in our particular bodies, in the midst of our particular lives, rooted as we are in the continuum of space and time. God is not limited to the constructs of either space or time, and His wisdom and workings often elude us as we try to make sense of what is happening in our lives. The Bible points out that His ways are not our ways, and His time is not our time. Our minds cannot even begin to fathom how great and wondrous His ways are. This is why things are not always what they seem to be and even the best-laid plans are sometimes overturned. Even when we feel we have been guided by our intuition every step of the way, we may find ourselves facing unexpected loss and disappointment. At times like these, we can find some solace in trusting that no matter how bad or just plain undesirable things look from our perspective, they are, in fact, in divine order. Our faith must become practical at times like these. I have a saying taped to my bedroom door that says, "EVERYTHING IS AS IT SHOULD BE. IT IS SO. IT CANNOT BE OTHERWISE." When I feel myself growing frustrated over the uncertainty of the future or my inability to control the present, I remember these words and softly whisper them to myself as a reminder that God is always in control, and as I continue to grow in Him and trust in Him, He will perfect everything that concerns me. With divine inspiration alive and well inside of me, I can press on confidently, knowing that God is in my corner, and He is always working on my behalf.

Faith is a choice. It is not a consequence of a person, place, or thing. It is a decision that we make when we arise each morning. However, it is this carnal part of us that suffers the greatest confusion and upset when the logic of events does not compute. And it is to this self that we must extend unconditional love, forgiveness, and compassion. In order to do this, we tap into our faith in God, holding the space of a tender authority, extending love and light to our spirits as a mother extends her love to a troubled child. Some of us seem to think that faith is something you're either born with or gifted with, but God has given each of us the capacity to trust Him and depend on Him because He created us in His own image.

We must learn to "be still" in the midst of our confusion. Not everything is for our understanding and comprehension. Our trust must lie in the fact that God has everything under control, that He who has hung the stars and the moon can do infinitely more than our minds can conceive and can bring us to and through every situation with exceeding joy.

There are many ways to access God's presence and strength in our lives as a calming force as we've explored: meditation, prayer, quiet time, Bible reading and developing healthy relationships. It is helpful to develop a regular practice that provides us access to this all-powerful, healing presence of divine inspiration, as it can be difficult to reach once we are in a stressful position if we have not already established a connection. Sometimes we feel lost amidst hard times or we feel that God is "distant". These feelings are usually a sign that we have to be more conscious than ever of God's presence in our lives when things are well in addition to the times we face challenges. He is a loving and patient God who wants communion with us, and we do ourselves a disservice by ignoring this love. The more connected we are with ourselves and God, the more we realize clearer, more divine vision and the security that comes with knowing that all the things of our lives, no matter how they appear, are in a state of divine and perfect order.

Chapter 3: Creating Divine Inspirations for Yourself

You can never solve a problem on the level on which it was created.
–Albert Einstein

Since God is the ultimate source of divine inspiration, it makes sense that we would need Him in order to create divine inspirations for ourselves. Without being connected to the source, we cannot reasonably expect to create and maintain divine inspirations in our lives. In this chapter, we'll explore several ways to create divine inspirations for ourselves such as discovering and developing our talents, committing to personal development, and consistently honoring our spirits.

Being happy and fulfilled is perhaps the best gift we can give to God and our loved ones. Think about how you behave to the people you love when you've had a really great day or when you wake up exceptionally happy. You're humming, you're smiling, you let people over in traffic, you give money to the homeless…all is right with the world. While we can't experience those kinds of highs every day of our lives, living an inspired life with purpose can free us to live in that place of happiness most days. In order to live in that place, we must first be completely aware of what things make us happy. This is not as simple as it seems considering that we are all complex beings who have a wide range of wants and needs. Furthermore, simply knowing what does or could contribute to our happiness is not enough if we do not make efforts to bring those things into our lives and manifest more of what we want. Once the discovery process is complete, we can begin actively pursuing our goals and dreams and leading fuller lives. When we have a purpose for each day, it's easier to accept life's challenges and to press forward towards the mark set before us.

Learning to love selflessly can be another challenge in our interpersonal development. Our society is one that places tremendous emphasis on self and on the pursuit of personal desires, regardless of the effect on

Divine Inspirations

others. However, if we truly want to live more purposeful lives, we have to respect others and treat them as people rather than a means to our end. God has instructed us to love one another as we love ourselves. If we are obedient and hide these instructions in our hearts, we'll slowly but surely find ourselves becoming kinder, gentler, and more patient with the imperfections of those around us.

We can also grow into people who are able to tell the truth, regardless of the consequences, because we know it is the right thing to do. For better or worse, many people believe that communicating in an honest and open way will not get them what they want. They have learned, instead, to play mind games or go on power trips in the service of their ego's agenda. People stuck in this backwards and inefficient style of communication can be difficult at best and completely destructive at worst. This kind of behavior only leads us deeper into confusion and conflict. The best way we can handle our challenges and our confusion is through open and honest communication. Lying, telling half-truths, and withholding the truth will all lead to debilitating emotions like resentment, betrayal, and hurt.

As with all relationships and situations in our lives, we must look within ourselves for both the source of our difficulties and the solution. God has given us introspection as a gift for uncovering the key to affecting change in the world around us. Our relationships are enhanced when we decide to take personal responsibility for our actions and our emotions. Only by disengaging, becoming still, and going within can we begin to see what has hooked us into the mess in the first place. The more we are able to do this, the more we can open ourselves up to our loved ones in healthy ways. In the light of our new awareness, the situation will untangle itself, and we will slowly break free with communication and truth as our guides.

What we often find at the core of our issues is unprocessed emotions that we can finally fully feel and release into the power that we find in prayer and meditation. This is important on your journey to living a divinely inspired life because the burial and denial of emotions can lead to a build up of negative emotion and can ultimately beset your life with unnecessary weight. Many of us go through life with a burden of pain and hurt beneath the surface of our emotions. Life's major painful events as well as simple daily offenses add up over time, and until we learn healthy ways to release our unhealthy emotions, we will continue to be victims of the past. For many of us, pain has set up shop in our souls and has made itself comfortable. We have hurt so long that we have forgotten that we should not be in pain, and cease making efforts to soothe the hurt.

With older and deeper hurts, we usually avoid facing our emotions at all costs. We pretend that we are "over it" and we insist on pressing forward in spite of a very real need to address what is happening inside of us. Unfortunately, this kind of issue typically rears its head at the most inopportune times. It may surface in unexpected ways, and we may even attribute the pain to something else. It's not until we afford ourselves still moments to reflect that we can really assess the source of the pain. Additionally, we can proactively identify the pain and take action towards healing it. It's easy to grow resistant to the process of sorting through the fractured parts of ourselves, but the trade off is very much worth it. Being able to lessen future hurts and free up our emotional energies can improve our lives dramatically.

Many of us have been trained to ignore or minimize our emotions. As children of God, we owe it to ourselves to honor each and every emotion we experience. This does not mean that we have to spend inordinate amounts of time dwelling on the past or on our negative experiences. This means that we consciously acknowledge what is happening inside of us and make informed and healthy decisions about how to move forward. We may not always have the emotional or mental resources to deal with our issues, and that is when we can turn to trained professionals or trusted friends to help us work through things. Whatever we choose, we can trust that God has not brought us to any place in our lives to leave us. He is full of grace, mercy, and patience and wants us to lead lives of abundance. He wants to heal our areas of brokenness and give us hope and a future.

Honoring Yourself and Your Needs

It's easy to go through this fast-paced world feeling as if you are being dragged through your weeks on the eye of a windstorm. Many of us go from one thing to another until we end up back at home in the evening with just enough time to wind down and go to sleep, waking up the next morning to begin the tornado of chaos once again. While this can be exhilarating for periods of time, a life lived entirely in disarray and hurry can be exhausting and unproductive. More importantly, it places us in the passenger's seat when we should be driving.

We were all made in the image of God who is the ultimate Creator. As such, we too are creators. I often say that we are the architects of our own lives. Pause for a moment to consider how many possibilities exist for you in your life. Many people live in a place of faithless limitation without ever really considering and appreciating that we have been given a plethora of choices for how to live our lives. This can include details such as what clothes we choose to put on each morning or more significant things such as our career paths or where we live. In spite of often feeling "stuck" or trapped in our current circumstances, we are free to create the lives that we want.

When we get caught up in our packed schedules and our many obligations, weeks can go by without us doing one thing we truly want to do or taking time to look at the bigger picture of our lives. Without taking time to consider the deeper implications of our choices, we run the risk of going through days, weeks, months, and years on autopilot. Taking a step back to examine our lives, praying for God's guidance, and asking ourselves if we are happy with the course we are on and making adjustments, puts us back in the driver's seat of our lives where we belong. When we take responsibility for charting our own course in life, we often go in an entirely different direction from the one laid out for us by society and familial expectations. This can be uncomfortable in the short term, but in the long term, we grow and expand by honoring our own inspirations and dreams and navigating our own course.

When I moved to California, I didn't have very much moral support. I remember being so excited about the possibilities of moving. I looked forward to making new friends, living in a new area, exploring a new city, and establishing a great career. Many of my friends and family members did not support my decision and were not hesitant in saying so. They told me that I should not make the move because I did not know anyone in California. They talked about how I would get lonely or overwhelmed and about the things they had heard. I never second-guessed my decision because I knew that moving was the right thing for me and that God would never lead me to a place where He would not protect me. In spite of being sure of my decision, I was hurt and confused by the need of others to belittle and criticize my decision to pursue my dreams and goals. In hindsight, moving to California was one of the best decisions I've made in my life, and I've grown exponentially as a person. The lesson I learned was that I am responsible for my life and my happiness. It is considerate to ponder how my decisions and actions may affect those around me, but it is necessary that I make decisions that are consistent with the things I value most, even if others can not appreciate those decisions.

Of course, examining the bigger picture of our lives doesn't always mean that we will find things that we are unhappy with, but monitoring our lives in this way keeps us connected with our greater purpose for living. Even if we want more extreme changes, the way to begin is to get off the road for long enough to see the forest for the trees and remember who we are and what we truly want. We must be diligent in not getting so caught up in the pursuit of our own desires that we forget to check in with God to be sure He is pleased with our paths. Ultimately, our goal should be to live in such a way that pleases Him. Without keeping our finger on His pulse, we can not be led by His Spirit. Once we take time to hear God and hear ourselves, we can take the wheel of our lives with confidence, driving the speed we want to go in the direction that is right for us. When our thoughts are scattered in several directions at once and we lose sight of our purpose, it is time to center ourselves.

When we center ourselves, we begin by acknowledging that we have become spread too thin and we are no longer unified with the larger purpose of our lives. Our thoughts might be out of sync with our feelings, and our actions may be out of sync with our values. We are usually given signs when we need to center ourselves. They include feeling out of control, not sleeping well, feeling resentful towards life, feeling as if God has left us, or feeling out of control. In addition, we may feel unfocused and not "alive" in our bodies. Centering ourselves is a healthy way of acknowledging all of the different energies, questions, and competing interests within us and reconciling them. With prayer and meditation, we can re-connect with the core of who we are and set about living in a more purposeful and inspired way. We naturally know how to center ourselves when we take a deep breath, for example, before making a big announcement or undertaking an important task. However, this process is not purely physical. We must apply the concept of the "deep breath" to our entire lives. Just like the inhale and exhale of our breathing, so is the flow of energy and attraction in our lives. We take in the circumstances, choices, people, and things around us, and we "exhale" our feelings, reflections, and thoughts about those things. Running the things we inhale through a "God filter" helps ensure that our "exhale" is our divine best. Our whole lives mirror this ebb and flow of energy that begins and ends with the essence of who we are in God. If we follow this ebb and flow, we can remain in harmony with ourselves and God. When we find we are out of harmony, we can always come back into balance with prayer and a concerted effort at revisiting our passions and purpose. When we pause to center ourselves we can imagine that we are gathering our straying thoughts and energies back into ourselves, the way we collect a stack of papers that has fallen off of a desk. We can also visualize ourselves back on a path of peace and fluid movement through our lives. From this place of centeredness, we can begin again, directing ourselves outward in a more intentional, divine way.

Emotional Detoxing

It's easy for those of us who have been to emotionally dark places to share the recovery part of our stories without sharing the muddy parts. Over time, I realized that my struggles and trials were nothing to be ashamed of. In fact, I should count these experiences as a nod to how courageous, powerful, and strong I am. Of course, in the midst of a trial, we rarely see ourselves as being conquerors, but we should. We'll touch on the concept of awakening your inner warrior in the face of a trial. With so many things happening around us, we often forget how important it is to listen to ourselves and our lives. They provide us with key insights on how we can live in the most efficient way possible. In this section, we'll discuss the importance of processing emotions, emotional detoxing, and adjusting to change. All of these things are essential to creating divine inspirations for yourself every day.

I've been in some very dark emotional places. I've been on the verge of an emotional breakdown of the monumental sort. I can remember times where I've begged God to take me out of my misery. Amidst such hopelessness, life is simply not worth living. There is no light at the end of the tunnel, and there is no rest for the weary soul. We've all had bad days, but there is a certain depth that comes to going through seasons of despair. It is not a fleeting dismay; it is a burden of certainty that things will never be well again.

Fortunately, God was gracious enough to spare my life. Psalm 34:18 says that God is close to the brokenhearted, and I believe it! I know that nothing but the grace of God was powerful enough to save me from myself during that time. I had done everything I knew how to pull myself up, but I was much too weak to fight the currents of sadness and darkness that engulfed me. My heart really goes out to people who fold under the pressures and trials of life. I often hear people refer to those who commit suicide as being "selfish" but for anyone who has ever been suicidal, it is easier to empathize with what those victims must face. Many of us underestimate the power of grief. I realize that it's not easy, but we are obligated as children of God to take care of ourselves. I literally felt my sanity and peace of mind leaving me, and I had to force myself to acknowledge what was happening with me emotionally. The process of emotional erosion can be a slow process, but the realizations are often sudden and sobering. I finally got to a place of having to talk to myself out loud and say, "I'm not well...I'm not mentally and emotionally well." Did it make me sound like a quack? Probably. But was it what I needed to fully acknowledge what was happening to me and help myself? Yes. The experts on recovery say that the first step is acknowledging that you have a problem, and so, that is where I began. As someone who has been there, I can offer insights on how to navigate the murky waters of extreme sadness and hopelessness. The most important thing is action. If you ever feel yourself slipping away, do something about it. Seek the help of a licensed and trained professional or find someone supportive to talk to about what's happening in your life. Spend some extra time praying and reading the Bible. Get out and exercise. Take a road trip. Do whatever you need to in order to regain your footing and feel better.

When we are weak, we know it's time to turn to God, for our weakness is made perfect in His strength. Oftentimes, we look to everyone and everything else to solve our problems instead of seeking God to discover the deeper meaning of what's happening in our lives. Our pain and suffering is needless when we can carry everything to God in prayer. The moment I surrendered was the moment I felt a peace that passes all understanding come over me, and I've been centered and happy since then. I realized that peace of mind is not to be taken for granted. It's a way of life that must be cultivated. I also realized that the mind is a powerful thing that must be subdued. God can give us the strength and courage to be bigger than any circumstance in our lives.

Anyone who has asked for divine guidance knows that it can be challenging to trust it when it comes. This is because divine guidance comes in many forms and it is sometimes hard to locate. We aren't sure if we are meant to trust our thoughts, our feelings, our dreams, or our intuitions to be the carriers of divine wisdom. We are not sure if advice from a friend is the form in which the guidance has come into the world, or if our own opinion is the source of wisdom we need to take seriously. The ability to sort all this out comes with trial and error, and the best way to learn to recognize divine guidance is to engage in the process of asking and receiving.

Sometimes when we ask for guidance, we already have a sense of what we want to hear. At such times, receiving guidance can be difficult, because we don't want to hear anything that appears to be in opposition to our desire. Therefore, one of the most important qualities we need to cultivate if we are to receive guidance is an open and objective mind. It helps to acknowledge what we want, and then to symbolically set it aside, making room for whatever wisdom comes through to us.

Cultivating an active relationship with God is the essential ingredient to being able to receive and trust guidance when it comes our way. We can make a daily practice of this through prayer and ongoing conversation with God. We can also use our journals, developing a relationship with God through the written word. As we request and receive guidance, we might take notes on our experiences. Over time we will begin to recognize when we were able to hear correctly and when we were not. In this way, we will gradually attune ourselves to our particular relationship with God. Begin to trust the guidance you are receiving, and soon you will find it flowing with ease.

Emotional Outbursts

Most of us have had the experience of holding back our emotions for such a long period of time that when they finally come out, we experience something that resembles a breakdown. For a certain period of time, the overwhelming flood of feelings coursing through our bodies consumes us, and we stop functioning. Often, these outbursts take us by surprise, welling up within us as we drive to or from work, watch a movie, or engage in some otherwise mundane task. We may feel like we do not know what triggered us, or if we do know, it does not make sense of our overpowering emotional response. This is because we are releasing feelings that have accumulated over a long period of time, and whatever inspired the release was just a catalyst for a much larger, much needed catharsis.

When we find ourselves in the midst of such an experience, it is important that we allow it to happen, rather than fight it or try to shut down. Wherever we are, we can try to find a private, safe place in which to let our feelings out. If we can not access such a place immediately, we can promise to set aside some time for ourselves at our earliest possible convenience, perhaps taking a day off work. The important thing is that we need to give our emotional system some much-needed attention. It is essential that we allow ourselves to release the pent-up emotions inside ourselves so that they do not create imbalances in our bodies and minds.

Once we are feeling better, we can make a plan to find a way to process our emotions more regularly. This can be done by employing a therapist or making a regular date to talk to a trusted friend. Making room in your life for tending your emotions on a regular basis will keep you healthy, balanced, and ready for life.

Many of us are familiar with the experience of waking up to the fact that our lives are no longer working the way we have set them up. Sometimes this is due to a shift occurring inside ourselves over time, and sometimes it is part of the larger shift that is currently affecting all humanity. Change is happening at such an increased rate that it is difficult to predict what the future holds. As a result, many of the old ways of planning out a life are no longer applicable, and if we cling to them we feel strangely out of tune with reality. If we are in tune with the world around us, we will begin to question ideas that just a few years ago seemed sensible.

In the simplest terms, the shift we are undergoing right now has to do with recognizing ourselves as being more than human and remembering that our earthly aspects are a very small part of who we are. In truth, we are multidimensional beings. When we begin to realize this, the life we planned for a limited conception of ourselves no longer fits. We must meet the needs and qualifications not only of our bodies but also of our souls. This realization dawns slowly for some and with the suddenness of a bolt of lightning for others, and we all must find the way that works for us to integrate this new and larger sense of self into our life plan.

Sometimes a drastic change feels right. Overnight we might decide to sell our home and move to another country or quit our job and begin a second career. Other times, we allow the changes to proceed slowly, beginning perhaps with allowing ourselves to dream and plan for a new life or just to ask God the deeper questions that encourage us to discover our true purpose in life. Either way, know that this process is a natural sign of the growth of a divine life, and trust it to guide you to the life of your dreams.

As we create the life of our dreams, we often reach a crossroads where the choices seem to involve the risk of facing the unknown versus the safety and comfort of all that we have come to trust. We may feel like a tightrope walker, carefully teetering along the narrow path to our goals, sometimes feeling that we are doing so without a net. What we must remember during these times is that God is the ultimate net! He will never leave nor forsake us, and He wants to see us grow and prosper. When we live our lives from a place of balance and trust in God, we may not always see our source of support, but we can know that it is there. God is often credited with moving in mysterious ways. I don't believe His ways are mysterious at all. They are simply higher than ours. If you created a computer program, its users may not entirely understand how the pieces fit together, but they would appreciate the functionality of your design. Likewise, as the great programmer of our universe, God's Hand remains at work in the lives of us who seek Him.

If we refuse to act only if we can see a safety net or a way out, we may be allowing what we perceive to be a net to become a trap as it creates a barrier between us and the freedom to pursue our goals. Change is inherent in life, so even what we have learned to trust can surprise us at any moment. Gaining a working understanding of the unfailing love and power of God can help us press forward in spite of uncertainty. Remove fear from the equation and then, without even wondering what is going to happen, we can devote our full attention to the dream that awaits us.

We attract support into our lives when we are willing to make those first tentative steps, trusting that God will provide exactly what we need. In that process, we can decide that whatever comes from our actions is only for our highest and best experience of growth. It may come in the form of a soft landing, an unexpected rescue or an eye-opening experience gleaned only from the process of falling. So rather than allowing our lives to be dictated by fear of the unknown, or trying to avoid pain, we can appreciate that sometimes we experience life fully when we are willing to trust God and possibly fall. And in doing so, we may just find that we have the wings to fly.

When we believe that there is a reason for everything, we are stepping out with God as our safety net, and we know we will make the best from whatever comes our way. Each of us is more than capable of making valuable contributions to the world, despite our fears and limitations and the uncertainty that holds us back. It is commonly accepted that it is impossible to make a difference without unlimited funding or free time, yet most healing, cleansing, and spreading of joy is accomplished in a matter of minutes. If we vow to make the world a better place one day at a time, the true significance of small good deeds reveals itself to us. We come to see that we can be of service without dedicating our lives to recognized charities or giving up the pleasures we enjoy. The warmth we feel when we help the world is only a tiny part of the affirmative transformations that take place when we make divine living a part of everyday existence.

We make our homes, workplaces, communities, and countries better and brighter when we think positive thoughts that echo outward, give donations of time or money, smile at people we meet, and lend to those in need of aid our assistance. As we learn, we inadvertently improve the world because we can only be truly involved when we are informed. Even enthusiastically sharing ideas with others generates positive energy that then serves as the motivation for more tangible change. Selfless and helpful deeds remind us that we exercise some degree of control over a world that can seem chaotic at times. Even the smallest of such deeds is a demonstration of the fact that we are capable of changing the world in a positive way. So much negative energy is generated by the suffering, pain, and close-mindedness we are regularly exposed to, but we can counteract it in a constructive way by thinking and acting divinely when opportunities to do so arise.

Helping the world often takes no more than a moment, just a wish for the world is a beautiful gesture and can be done by even the busiest of people effortlessly. The gift you give each day need not be grand or attention-worthy because the broader benefits are the same no matter the literal repercussions. Once a day, you can affect reality, and you can reap the rewards of knowing that you are making the world a better place, day by day.

The first step to getting what you want in life is knowing what you want. This may sound obvious, but a surprising number of us are going through life without really coming to terms with the truth of what we want. There are many reasons for this, and they range from parental influences that curb our imaginations to external factors that curb our ability to take action. We may feel that getting too caught up in exploring our deepest desires is wasted energy when it seems we want things beyond our grasp. This is a very practical attitude and has its benefits, but it can be safely balanced with a more imaginative and unlimited approach to the question of what we want. I'm always disheartened when I hear people speak of dreams and hopes as far off impossibilities that could never be realized. The difference between the people who live their dreams and those who don't is choice. People who are living their dreams do not magically stumble into a life of purpose, fulfillment, and joy. It requires choice and a willingness to press toward the mark.

Perhaps you are 40 years old and find within yourself a desire to be a ballet dancer. You see the impracticality and seeming impossibility of this idea, so you reject it without exploring it. But perhaps you should allow yourself to feel this desire and perhaps even take a dance class. Allowing yourself to participate in ballet in small ways may provide inspiration that leads you in a new direction in life. And time spent doing what you want to do is never wasted because it generates energy that can fuel the rest of your life.

You can begin to uncover and discover what you want by doing a simple, timed writing exercise. Set your timer for 15 minutes and write without stopping, starting every sentence with the words "I want." Writing without stopping for a set period of time enables your inner voice to override your inner censor and helps to unearth buried dreams. It also creates a feeling of relief in the mind, heart, and body. This exercise can also be practiced orally, alone or in the company of a friend. You might try doing this exercise every morning for a week, looking back at the end of the week to see what has come up. Sometimes the simple act of expressing a want actually releases it, while other yearnings retain their energy, asking us to pay attention. When we pay attention to what we want, we are that much closer to getting it.

More On Detoxing

When we want to start with a clean slate in life, one way is to cleanse our bodies. Detoxifying can be done in many ways and for many reasons, depending on our specific goals. You may feel a physical need for cleansing, or a spiritual one where you would cleanse the areas of the body that correspond to your current life challenges. If you feel, for instance, that your inner self is not shining through as you would like, you may want to do a bathing detox to clean the skin of impurities so that you can radiate your inner health like a newly washed stained-glass window that lets the light shine through more brilliantly.

No matter how healthy and conscious our habits are, our bodies move with the cycles of life, which means that our cells sometimes need to fall like leaves from the trees before they can regenerate and be renewed. Just as we need to wash our bodies to remove the buildup of natural processes and contact with the world around us, we need to clean our bodies from the inside as well. This can be physical or spiritual. So you may want to detoxify your blood or digestive system, or target specific buildup such as plaque or metals. Our bodies are temples, and they should be honored as sacred. These unique gifts from God are vessels that allow us to move through life, and they should be treated like delicate flowers that need our attention to reach their full potential of beauty.

The first days of a detoxification process may bring to mind an image of the dust that gets stirred up during spring cleaning. We often feel worse before we feel better, but that may be God's way of showing us the benefits by contrast. We live in a world of dualities, so we may need to experience both sides of a situation in order to find our perfect balance. Once the impurities have been cleansed, we can experience a sense of lightness or clarity of vision and purpose.

Being Gentle With Yourself

During those times when our lives are filled with what seems to be constant change and growth, it is important to remember that we need to be gentle with ourselves. Since it can be easy to use our energy to keep up with the momentum of our lives, we may not be aware of the fact that we are much more likely to run ourselves down. When things seem to be moving quickly, it is especially essential that we make a point to slow down and be gentle with ourselves.

It might be difficult to notice what is happening to us for we may be so caught up in the whirlwind of our lives that we lose sight of the direction in which things are heading. Being gentle with ourselves doesn't mean that we don't accomplish things. Instead it means that we honor ourselves on an ongoing basis and take care of the needs of our bodies. In today's fast paced society, many of us are straining our minds and bodies attempting to be everything to everyone at all times. It's no wonder that we experience such high levels of stress and anxiety. When we become so concerned with busyness that we ignore our spirits, we begin a destructive process that will eventually lead to our bodies shutting down. I'm sure you've heard that you have to love yourself before you can love anyone else. Well, I submit that we have to honor and care for ourselves before we can honor or care for another as well. Self care and personal attention are important in leading a healthy and balanced life. This means different things to different people. For instance, it could mean getting a physical check up; taking herbs or vitamins; or getting extra sleep. Putting our energy into ourselves in this way helps create space for a more positive, loving, and accepting view of our lives. By setting the intention to do so, we will be more cognizant of our energy levels on a daily basis and more able to replenish them as needed. Our bodies respond in positive ways when we treat them well. I once read a great quote on health: "If you neglect your health, it will go away." This idea drives home the message that our health is one of the most precious assets we have, and we must honor it as such.

The more we are able to treat our bodies with gentleness, the more tenderness and compassion we will call forth into our lives. Learning to understand and pay attention to what our self needs will in turn allow us to fill our lives with unlimited loving and divine energy and to truly take care of the things that mean the most to us.

Divine Inspirations

Moving Out Of Your Comfort Zone

When our lives are going well, and sometimes even when they aren't, we may find ourselves feeling very attached to the status quo of our existence--life as we know it. It is a very human tendency to resist change as though it were possible to simply decide not to do it, or have it in our lives. But change will come and the status quo will go, sooner or later, with our consent or without it. You have probably heard the saying that the only constant is change. We may find at the end of the day that we feel considerably more empowered when we find the courage to ally ourselves with the inevitable force of change, rather than working against it. As with many other things in our lives, our response to the things that happen to us can either serve us or debilitate us. It was Sukuma who said that the wind does not break a tree that bends. If we can learn to bend in facilitative ways to the change that visits us, then we can enjoy richer, fuller lives instead of being "snapped" like a twig that cannot withstand the force of the wind.

Of course, we don't want to go about changing things at random, without regard to whether they are working or not. There is a time and place for stability and the preservation of what has been gained over time. In fact, the ability to stabilize and preserve what is serving us is part of what helps us to survive and thrive. The problem comes when we become more attached to preserving the status quo than to honoring the divine possibilities of growth and change. For example, if we allow a situation we are in to remain stagnant simply because we are comfortable, it may be time for us to summon up the courage to challenge the status quo.

This may be painful at times, or surprisingly liberating, and it will most likely be a little of both. Underneath the discomfort, we will probably find excitement and energy as we take the risk of unblocking the natural flow of energy in our lives. We are fortunate to have a God who is loving and patient and will send a Great Comforter to help us through our difficult times. The process of letting go of the need for things to never change is like dismantling a dam inside ourselves, because most of the work involves clearing our own inner obstacles so that the divine river of our life can flow unobstructed. Once we remove the obstacles, we can simply go with the flow, trusting the changes that follow.

As human beings we often have a tendency to fight against using our natural gifts. Many stories of success start with an individual who is ignoring the call of his or her inborn abilities. There are many possible reasons for this resistance, from fear that the calling will be too difficult to a disbelief in the very work one is being asked to do. We may feel too small, too distracted by other people's ideas about what we should do, or too uninformed. Whatever the case, the resistance to actualizing ourselves has very concrete consequences, and many of us have been called out of hiding by an illness or a twist of fate that unequivocally dismantled our resistance. In other words, God knocks, and if we don't answer He knocks louder and eventually sends situations that can not be ignored. When I was preparing the manuscript of this book, I often felt fear and uncertainty. I cowered at the thought of being a published author with my words and thoughts bare for everyone to read and scrutinize. I asked God to give the gift and task to another more willing servant, but I slowly began to realize that my resistance came from a deep need to remain comfortable in my life instead of appreciating my ongoing growth process. I remember feeling overwhelmed with the visions and plans God had given me, but He assured me that He would not leave me without provision. I finally committed to working on this book, and while I had some challenges in the writing process, I grew exponentially. One of the reasons change is so important is because it helps us to grow. We were put here to evolve into completely self-actualized, divine beings. Imagine a small child who grew older but still insisted on drinking from a bottle and wearing diapers. What would it mean for a high school teenager to drink from a bottle and wear diapers? The idea seems absurd to us, but we look just as absurd when we cling desperately to the status quo instead of welcoming change and examining the many ways it can help us grow.

The first step on the journey to our calling in life is to listen to God's voice and our internal voices and respond to the opportunities and challenges knocking at the door. As we do, the symptoms and anxieties of fear of the unknown that have haunted us will fade into the background, replaced by opportunities, both big and small, to open the door to what we are truly here to do. Most of us have the feeling that we are here to accomplish something big in our lives, and if we haven't done something that fits the bill we may feel as if we are waiting. We may feel incomplete, or empty, as if our lives don't yet make sense to us, because they don't line up with our idea of major accomplishment. In some cases, this may be because we really are meant to do something that we haven't yet done. But in most cases, we can let ourselves off the hook with the realization that just being here, being ourselves, is enough. Some people are so concerned with doing something so grand that they miss the value of being. God has called us to be, do, and have abundance. Notice that "be" was first in that list. We occasionally cross paths with people who simply are remarkable. To look at their resumes or accomplishments, we would not be exceptionally impressed, but to be in their presence, we quickly recognize that the person is divine. Simple things go a long way in living a divine life. The person who has simply learned to be bigger than life's adversities has accomplished something great.

As we live our lives in this world, we share our energy and our spirit with the people around us in numerous ways. Our influence touches their lives and, through them, touches the lives of many more people. When we strive to live our lives to the fullest and to become our true selves, we are doing something big on an inner level, and that is more than enough to make sense of our being here on this planet at this time. There is no need to hold ourselves to an old idea in the back of our minds that we need to make headlines or single-handedly save the world in order to validate our existence.

We can each look within our hearts to discover what is true for us, what gives our lives meaning, and what excites us. We can release ourselves from any pressure to perform that comes from outside of our inner sense of purpose. Staying in tune with our own values and living our lives in tune with our own vision is all we need in order to fulfill our time here. Our lives are a process of becoming so that we cannot help but cocreate with God; being who we are, responding to each moment as it comes, we can trust that this is enough.

Unleashing Your Inner Warrior

There are certain personality archetypes that we all carry within us, such as the inner child, the lover, and the nurturer. Some of these archetypes present themselves strongly, while others lay fallow. For example, there is an inner warrior in each one of us, but in some of us this warrior is underdeveloped to the point that we are unable to stand up for ourselves, even when necessary. We avoid conflict, say yes when we mean no, and suffer from low self-esteem. There can be many reasons for this. We may have grown up with a parent whose warrior aspect was overdeveloped, and we responded by repressing ours completely to subconsciously create an energetic balance. On the other hand, we may have grown up with parents in whom this aspect was dormant, so we never learned to awaken it in ourselves.

A warrior is someone with the strength to stand up for what he or she believes; someone who perseveres in the face of challenges and obstacles; someone who speaks and acts in the service of an ideal; someone who protects those who are too weak to fight for themselves. Regardless of the reasons for an underdeveloped inner warrior, you may begin to notice the lack of its fiery, protective presence and wish to awaken it. You may need to stand up for yourself in a certain relationship or situation, or you may have a vision you want to realize, and you know you will need the courage, energy, and strength of a warrior to succeed. Similarly, if you find that you often feel scared, anxious, or powerless, rousing this sleeping ally may be just the antidote you need. I realized at the beginning of last year that my inner warrior needed to be awakened. I had gotten my first spiritual prompts to move into production, and the very thought overwhelmed me. I knew that while there was great potential for success, prosperity, and touching lives, there was also a tremendous risk of challenges, resistance, and frustrations. I realized that I had reached a sort of cross roads where I would have to decide to be strong and vigilant for my cause or to retreat at the first sign of trouble. I chose to awaken my inner warrior.

One excellent way to cultivate the presence of your inner warrior is to choose a role model who embodies the qualities of bravery, strength, and vitality. This person could be a character in a myth, movie, or book, or a historical or living person you admire. Simply close your eyes each day and contemplate the quality of energy that attracts you to this person, knowing that the same potential lives within you. Confirm for yourself that you are capable of handling this energy responsibly, and stoke the fire of your own inner courage. When you are faced with trials, awaken your inner warrior. Instead of shrinking from life, grab it by the horns. Most folks are much stronger and braver than they realize. The personal growth we realize when we commit to our goals is miraculous, and our inner warrior acts as a sidekick of sorts to help us get through difficult times victoriously.

Trusting Self

Throughout our lives, we will encounter individuals who presume to know what is best for us. You probably know that friend or family member who seems to always have the answers for what you should do in spite of not completely having their own lives in order. The insights they offer cannot compare, however, with the powers of awareness and discernment that already exist within us. From birth we are blessed with wisdom that cannot be learned or unlearned. It exists whether or not we acknowledge it because it is a gift given to us by a loving God before we chose to experience existence on the earthly plane. Yet for all its permanence, it is vital that we value and honor this incredible element of the self. It is when we do not use our inborn wisdom that we begin to doubt our personal truths and are driven to outside sources of information because we are afraid. Have you ever asked someone for advice even though you had a feeling of what you should do deep down inside? Those hunches and unexplained pulls we receive are divine. The more in tune we are with God, the more clarity we can have on the direction our lives should take. What we know to be true in our hearts is invariably true, and we discover how intensely beautiful and useful self-trust can be when we recognize the power of our wisdom.

Inner wisdom is not subject to the influences of the outside world, which means that it will never demand that we surrender our free will or counsel us to act in opposition to our values. God is not the author of confusion, and He will give us insights into our lives that cannot be explained in logical ways. He will also give us a value system by which to live. Our values are the guiding hands that persuade our actions and ultimately our lives. The wisdom of the truth we live in each day can serve to be the voice of assurance we need to live truthfully each day. We benefit from this inspiration when we open ourselves to it, letting go of the false notion that we are less qualified than others to determine our fate. Who could possibly be more of an expert on your life than you? The wisdom inside of us is the source of our discernment and our ability to identify blessings in disguise. When we are unsure of who to trust, how to respond, or what we require, the answers lie in our inner wisdom. It knows where we are going and understands where we are coming from, taking this into account though it is not a product of experience but rather a piece of our connection to God, in all of His divine intelligence.

In the whole of your existence, no force you will ever encounter will contribute as much to your ability to do what you need to do and be who you want to be as your natural wisdom. Through it, you reveal your growing consciousness to God and discover the true extent of your strength. If you heed this wisdom with conviction and confidence, the patterns, people, and fears that held you back will be dismantled, paving the way for you to fulfill your truest potential. Most people agree that a more peaceful world would be an ideal situation for all living creatures. However, we often seem stumped as to how to bring this ideal situation into being. If we are to have true peace in this world, each one of us must find it in ourselves first. If we don't like ourselves, for example, we probably won't like those around us. If we are in a constant state of inner conflict, then we will probably manifest conflict in the world. If we have fighting within our families, there can be no peace in the world. We must shine the light of inquiry on our internal struggles, because this is the only place we can really create change. The great philosophers advised that we "know self" because without doing so, our attempts at living life will be mediocre at best. You may have heard Ghandi's call to be the change you want to see in the world. Without first examining ourselves and committing to our own excellence, we can not create divine lives or assist others in doing the same.

When we initiate the process of looking inside ourselves for the meaning of peace, we will begin to understand why it has always been so difficult to come by. This in itself will enable us to be compassionate toward the many people in the world who find themselves caught up in conflicts both personal and universal. We may have an experience of peace that we can call up in ourselves to remind us of what we want to create, but if we are human we will also feel the pull in the opposite direction—the desire to defend ourselves, to keep what we feel belongs to us, to protect our loved ones and our cherished ideals, and the anger we feel when threatened. This awareness is important because we cannot truly know peace until we understand the many tendencies and passions that threaten our ability to find it. Peace necessarily includes, even as it transcends, all of our primal energy, much of which has been expressed in ways that contradict peace. We must understand the things that get in the way of peace before we can successfully remove them.

Being at peace with ourselves is not about denying or rejecting any part of ourselves. On the contrary, in order to be at peace we must be willing and able to hold ourselves, in all our complexity, in a full embrace that excludes nothing. God loves us unconditionally, and we must extend this same love to ourselves. This is perhaps the most difficult part for many of us, because we want so much to disown the negative aspects of our humanity. Ironically, though, true peace begins with a willingness to take responsibility for our humanity so that we might ultimately transform it in the light of God's love.

Chapter 4: Cultivating a Divine Environment

Nobody can go back and start a new beginning, but anyone can start today and make a new ending. –Maria Robinson

We've all heard the saying that you're a product of your environment. I subscribe to this belief, and it is essential to creating a divine life. By structuring our lives in divine ways, we can build a support system of sorts that will enhance the wonderful parts of our lives and strengthen the weaker areas. Our environment can be defined in many different ways, but for our purposes, we'll explore four important areas: your home, your car, your workplace, and your church. These are the places we typically spend the majority of our time. Some of you may notice that relationships, in the romantic context, were left off of the list. That is because we'll spend time discussing relationships at length later in the book. Believe it or not, there is a divine approach to each of these aspects of our lives. With a little effort, we can develop healthier, more abundant lifestyles that continue to feed and nurture our spirits, thus making us better human beings.

Home

Your home is probably the most important place in your life. Few people understand how important their choice of home is. Many of us sort of accept our homes as they are and allow ourselves to haphazardly go from place to place without making choices that are consistent with honoring our spirits and our long-term goals for ourselves. However, when we consider that our homes are supposed to be an escape from the cares of the world and a place to replenish and rest, we can approach our living quarters with the right attitude.

Sometimes our lives are so busy that we treat our homes as if they were impersonal places that we merely pass through. We rush out into the world in the morning, and we are away until sundown when we stumble back in, tired and downtrodden from a day of activity. Imagine what it would be like to come home to a beautifully decorated home. Picture yourself stepping into this beautiful place and immediately feeling a sense of calm. As you walk around, you put your things away, and you sit for a moment to relax and allow your mind to settle. You feel the stress and tension of the day melting away, and you feel a sense of serenity wash over you. Then you find your family members and begin greeting them and exchanging stories about the day. You are happy and satisfied with life, and you continue to unwind and enjoy the comforts of being home.

Does this sound like your home? If not, it can! Too many of us see a wonderful home life as some elusive goal that can never be achieved. Creating a wonderful and divine home life takes work. It requires a serious commitment to maintaining a certain standard in the home. We can make certain that our homes truly feel like our sanctuaries by taking the time to tend to them like gardens. We all know that gardens are not something we can set up and then abandon. One must tend to it by watering it, removing the weeds, and nourishing the soil. Likewise, we have to approach the care of a divine home life in the same way. We can not set a great home in motion and then leave it to its own devices. As life happens and as we grow, we must be sure that our homes continue to provide us with the safety and peace we desire. We have to spread love around our homes. We have to remove any discord and negativity, and we have to allow God's spirit to be present in our homes. Without proper care, our homes can not offer us the beauty of their blooms. When we take the time to treat a home like a beloved oasis, we can shift their energy from merely being a place to being a haven of safety and replenishment of our souls.

Take a moment to think about the homes you've visited. Some were dirty, some were clean, some had a glamorous feel, while others felt more "earthy". We often are able to learn many profound things about a person based on how she or he lives and the choices they made about their home. After all, second to work, most people spend the majority of their time at home. With so much time spent there and with the climate of the home being entirely up to us, unlike work, we can see how important the home is to helping us live divine lives.

Consider that homes are the outer reflections of the spirit that lives within. Some people may find this analysis a little too "deep" but if we examine it, we'll see the validity of it. Have you ever been around a person who has a spastic, uncentered energy about them? More often that not, these people are unorganized, and their environments reflect the chaos going on inside of them. Likewise, we often encounter people who seem more "together" and responsible, and we see that they are typically organized. These kinds of basic things are a reflection of what is going on inside of us. Our environments are an accidental canvas of the paintbrush of our minds. When we feel that the current environment clashes with how we perceive ourselves, it can keep us from fully allowing our light to shine. Perhaps this issue is not organization. Maybe the issue is color. Typically, people with more lively personalities gravitate to bright, bold colors while more reserved types go for the muted tones. Regardless of our tastes in design, the point is that our homes should be a reflection of the most alive and happy parts of ourselves, whatever that may be.

Updating our homes to reflect our inner landscape need not involve massive redecorating or a large financial investment. Small things can go a long way toward creating a divine environment. Something as simple as putting up more pictures of loved ones around the house can help create an environment in which we feel loved and connected to those we love. Perhaps you have some trinkets that a loved one who passed away has given you, and you've been keeping them tucked away in a drawer. Finding a way to honor that person's spirit in your home is a great way to make your environment more personal.

Small repairs are another great way to create a divine environment. Does that leaky faucet annoy you? Are you sick and tired of looking at the scuff marks on the door? Take some time to correct these annoyances and you'll find that your home is more enjoyable. Organizing and cleaning is another low-cost way to remove chaos and unrest from our homes and introduce more calm. Lovingly rejuvenating our personal space can become a creative project that increases the flow of good vibes throughout our lives and gives us an opportunity to become more aware of what we have and how we can best use what we have. We can do something good and donate old things to charity, opening space for newness to enter. Creating more peace and happiness in our homes can be as simple as finding a specific location for mail and keeping it organized so that it's easy to sort through. We can also create peace by placing plants and artwork throughout the home to make it inviting and pleasing to the eye.

Simplifying and beautifying our space lets our imagination and energy roam free. Our homes can be a great inspiration to us. We can choose to prioritize our homes, making them the true heart of our family's activities. We can find solace, peace, and rest in our homes when we treat them like the thrones of our reign. Once we give our homes their proper place, we are free to focus on the things that really matter like time with loved ones, and achieving our goals.

Car

You may not think of your car as a place to create a little divine inspiration, but as you set about living a more purposeful and happy life, you will find new opportunities to enjoy small pleasures and maximize your growth potential. Henry David Thoreau said that the man is richest whose pleasures are cheapest. That idea points to the fact that when we are able to find a little slice of happiness in every area of our lives, we can ultimately cultivate joy and peace. After all, there is silver lining in all that we do. It is up to us to find it.

Think about how much time you spend in your car. With society growing increasingly more busy and with the trend of trying to squeeze more productivity into the same 24 hours, we can see how our time spent in our cars has increased significantly. I never knew it was possible to drive so many hours and not go very many places until I moved to Los Angeles. The city is spread out, and in a typical day, I may spend anywhere from one to four hours in my car. That time can be a waste or an investment, depending on how I choose to approach it. In your car, there are often many things competing for your attention. There is the most important thing, the road, but there is also the phone, the radio, the temperature, other passengers, and the scenery. It's easy to see how something as simple as a trip to grocery store could leave you mentally overloaded.

Let's examine some of the ways to alleviate some of that stress and make your car time more enjoyable. First, let's consider what should be done when you get into the car. Always be sure to wear your safety belt and be sure that other passengers are wearing theirs. Then, set the temperature to something comfortable, not too hot and not too cold so as to eliminate constant fidgeting with the controls. Then, check your mirrors to be sure you can see around your vehicle. Once you start the car, decide on the music or radio station you want to listen to and set an appropriate volume. In the past, I've been guilty of starting the car, pulling out and then trying to play with the radio, the air conditioning, and my mirrors while driving. These things should be taken care of prior to beginning the trip. I know this sounds obvious to the seasoned driver, but you would be surprised how many of us could use a friendly reminder of the basics.

Also, consider the little things that can be done to improve your commute. I have an inspirational quote taped to the inside of my visor so every time I pull it down, I'm inspired. I've also put pictures of loved ones there as a reminder that I am loved and that there are wonderful people in my life to whom I may give love. Another little pleasure of mine is air fresheners. Each time I get into my car, I get a whiff of freshness in the scent of peach, watermelon, green tea, or mango. I also make it a point to get my car washed when it needs it. Driving a clean car that smells nice is a small pleasure of mine. Another favorite car activity is listening to books on CD. I have been able to finish "reading" many books by picking up the CD version at the library or purchasing it at a book store and enjoying it in my car. I notice that I am less tense and in a better state of mind when I arrive at my destination after having listened to something interesting on the way.

In many cities across America, you are what you drive. While I don't believe our individual identity or self-worth should be in any way attached to what we drive, I do believe that we should be good stewards of all we have been given, including transportation. This may seem like a simple concept, but in the same way that we often feel better about ourselves when we look great, we can develop the same feelings about our cars, whether we drive a clunker or a luxury vehicle.

Work

In America, we have a reputation for being workaholics. We work 40-80 hours a week, and we do not take vacations nearly as often as we should. Getting off work, even for important things, is a challenge sometimes, and we are all about productivity. With this trend, it is important that we maintain balance. We have become so passionate about our pursuit of money, cars, homes, and career success that we have lost sight of important things like our families, our personal ambitions, and our health. I can not say that I have never been in this category. Even during the writing of this book, I was busy producing and directing a stageplay, producing a young women's empowerment conference, starting a business, and keeping up with friends, family, and personal goals. To say that I was busy is an understatement. I enjoy having a fast-paced life, but I have to remind myself that balance is important. For every hour of work, there should be an hour of non-work – time spent with family, time spent alone, time spent playing, time spent enjoying life.

With our relentless work schedules and our emphasis on productivity, you would think that many of us were head over heels in love with our careers and the work that we do. However, job dissatisfaction is a growing trend in corporate America. The schedules, the office politics, and the job structure have created an underlying resentment and frustration with the average worker. A happy workplace is a rare find, but there are things you can do to create divine inspirations at work. I happen to love the career I've crafted for myself, but before all of this came to be, I was the typical disgruntled worker in the typical company. I wanted more, and I was frustrated with the stagnation I felt at my workplace and in my career. I realized that if I wanted to truly be happy at work, or anywhere else for that matter, I would have to commit to maintaining mental equanimity and pursuing happiness wherever it was to be found.

When you wake up on Monday mornings, what is your first thought? Is it dread of going to work and having to fight the battle of a new week? If so, perhaps you need a shift of perspective to help you gain a more balanced attitude toward work. How do you feel when you walk into work? Happy? Sad? Mad? Tired? Our emotions are an intuitive thermostat of our lives, and it is very important that we give them their due by listening when our emotions are telling us things. If you feel overwhelmed by the very thought of going to work, this may be a sign that some things need to change or that you need to make special efforts to create divine inspirations at work.

Are you grateful for your job? Gratitude is important in helping us gain perspective on things in our lives. What if you lost your job today? How would you feel? If you would be anxious about the lack of income, then ask yourself what you're doing to create an emergency fund and peace of mind. If you would be happy, ask yourself why. Is it because you've outgrown your job? Is it because you work for a supervisor who is disrespectful and condescending? Is it because you are under compensated for your worth? These are all things that need to be explored at length. If you would be disappointed to lose your job because it's not so bad after all, then perhaps you should try taking a different approach to work.

For many people, a change of scenery would be a tremendous help. This could mean transferring to a different office, spending some time working from home, or working outside at a park one or two days a week. If you believe you may simply need to shake things up a bit, try talking with someone above you about a change of schedule or a change of environment. If you can't go to the change of environment, try bringing a change of environment to you. Consider putting plants, artwork, or photos of your loved ones in your work space to make it more personal and more comfortable. I remember a time when I worked in a stuffy office with equally stuffy people. I felt myself growing more rigid and tense over the first weeks I was there. I decided to bring in photos of my puppy, my parents, and far off exotic places to lighten the mood at my desk. Not only did these things make me smile, they helped me to keep things in perspective.

There are other times when we simply grow bored with doing the same job, in the same space, with the same people year after year. If you are feeling the burden of monotony, this may be a sign that you have outgrown your job. If the management in your company is not tapping you for a promotion, then consider how you could make that happen for yourself. Too often, we think we should be entitled to a raise or a promotion simply because we've gotten up every morning and shown our faces at the offices for a certain number of days. However, we have to take a more proactive approach to getting the things we want. Remember that your employer did not hire you to be a warm body filling a seat; they hired you to do an efficient job at completing your assigned tasks so until you are able to do your job and do it well, you can't truly be upset at what appears to be a snub on the part of your office's administration.

How good are you at what you do? Do you give it 100% every day when you come in? Are you cordial and pleasant to your co-workers? Do you bring your problems at home to work? Do you take "leisurely" lunches on the company's time? Do you steal supplies from the office? All of these things have to be considered in making an honest assessment of why you may be unhappy with your workplace. If you are not giving your best to your job, you can not reasonably expect your work to give its best to you. Once you begin working at full capacity, you'll be able to make an honest assessment of what your strengths are and how to go about using those in a way that can fulfill you and increase your job satisfaction. Believe it or not, employees who give their work 100% of their efforts report being more satisfied than those who don't. Holding back your best is tiring and requires more effort than doing your best.

If you are doing your best and working efficiently and you are still unhappy, you may need to consider a career change. Perhaps your line of work is not your passion or maybe you have outgrown your position or your employer and need to move on. In today's working world, few people stay with the same company for years and years. There is much more career mobility available to the working man or woman and this has been both a gift and a curse. One of the principles of divine inspiration is creating the life you want to live. By being able to move more effortlessly in and out of positions, you are freed up to grow in a progressive and evolutionary way. Those who despise change and uncertainty would argue that the new climate in corporate America lends itself to instability for the working person with a family who needs a steady income. In reply to that, I say that there is no such thing as job stability any more. There is certainly the illusion that a traditional 9-5 office job would offer more stability than a creative job, but as many who have been laid off can testify, employers are no longer loyal to their employees. There are many employees who have been working with one company for ten or twenty years and show up at work to find that their desks have been cleared or that the company is letting them go. So, we should be careful not to be lulled into the idea that there is stability in working for someone else. The best thing we can do is develop the skills and talents necessary to survive, regardless of how the job market may fluctuate. This could extend to owning a small business on the side or developing a larger company that will provide true independence. One of my favorite quotes by Helen Keller is below. Consider it where your career is concerned.

Security is mostly a superstition. It does not exist in nature, nor do the children of men as a whole experience it. Avoiding danger is no safer in the long run than outright exposure. Life is a daring adventure or nothing at all.

For a long time, I was bored and frustrated with the jobs I was working. They were often monotonous, boring, and uninteresting. I rarely learned anything new or helpful, and I often found myself dreading going to work and looking forward to days off. While there are the typical ups and downs of working, work should not be drudgery! In America, many of us spend a significant amount of time working. With so much of our energy and attention being given to work, we should make every effort to align our work with our passions and things that fulfill us. When I began the process of creating divine inspirations for myself in my career, I asked myself some important questions to gain some insight on what was important to me.

Consider these questions as you assess your current position or look for a new one:

-If money were no object, what would you do each day?
-How did you end up working in your current profession?
-What do you love about your current job?
-What do you dislike about your current job?

-If you had to take a 30% pay cut, would you stay at your current job/company?
-If you could have any job within your company, what would it be and what would be required in order for you to get that job?
-Do you get to use your natural talents on your job each day?
-Are you growing as a professional at your current job?
-Would you be a happier person if you were doing a different job?
-Do you find your work rewarding on any level?
-Do you like your supervisor?
-Do you like the company you work for?
-Are you consistently stressed out at the end of your work day?

Regardless of your working situation or your career aspirations, answering these questions honestly can help you gain a better idea of what direction you should be headed. Notice that there were no questions on the list about making more money. This was done intentionally. The problem with making career decisions solely on income potential is that money is not the only factor that determines happiness in work. I realize that most people assume that if they were making millions of dollars each year, they would be happy. However, the truth of the matter is that while income and a comfortable lifestyle are both important, there are other things that are just as important. Being happy, spending time with family, and enjoying life are also important in choosing a job or career. What good is millions of dollars if you have no time to spend it or no one to share it with? The pursuit of material things in our society has clouded our judgment of what is truly important. I enjoy having nice things as much as the next person, but over time, I have come to realize and appreciate that there is no substitute for peace of mind or happiness. All the money in the world can not buy you quality time with your spouse or your children nor can it buy you fulfillment or a sense of purpose.

So, in your creation of divine inspirations at work, remember to keep things in perspective and don't lose sight of what is important now and how the decisions you make today will affect you tomorrow. Much of who you are is reflected in your work and how you approach it so be sure there is a touch of divinity in your life's work.

Church

For many Christians, church is like a home away from home. Countless hours are devoted to church activities, service, and fellowship with the church family. The Bible tells us not to forsake fellowship with other believers. Many Christians draw inspiration, motivation, and a sense of belonging from their relationships with their pastors or spiritual leaders as well as the congregations to which they belong.

I strongly encourage fellowship of this sort because it can achieve many functions in creating divine inspirations as well as developing ourselves into more well-rounded, loving human beings. The act of being grouped is one that is a function of our growth. As I mentioned earlier, we've all heard the saying that no man is an island. This is true. Being grouped and finding healthy ways to relate to others in a group setting is good for us emotionally and mentally. It gives us an opportunity to see that we are not alone in this big world, with all of its problems and temptations. We can also appreciate the bonds that can be formed in developing safe friendships and relationships. By being willing to accept others as they are and to be accepted in return, we are able to create divine relationships. All of these elements of grouping are enhanced several times over when they are done with people of God. While no church is perfect, the beauty of the church is that it is a place under God's covering. It should be a place where we can gain acceptance and receive forgiveness.

However, it would be misleading of me to oversimplify the church experience without making suggestions for creating divine inspirations at church. We touched briefly on religious tolerance in an earlier chapter, and we will discuss concepts such as unconditional love and forgiveness later in the chapter on relationships. For now, let's examine the church and some of the ways we can go about making our church experience better through divine inspirations.

Many of us have been members of our respective churches for years. We've grown, transitioned, and evolved in this setting, and church is often one of the most comfortable and familiar things in our lives, primarily because of the perceived stability associated with it. A level of comfort and security at church is a wonderful, affirming thing, especially for the babe in Christ who is still learning what it means to enjoy Christian fellowship. However, many of us have been lulled into a rut of sorts by the comfort of routine. We attend the same services every week, we participate in the same Bible study every week, and we do the same things between services every week. The spiritual growth in these situations is stunted. Sometimes repetition and boredom can open the door for distractions. When we're bored, we often become consumed with details that are unimportant or we begin knit picking with others as a subconscious way to keep ourselves entertained. This is why staying busy and maintaining an awareness of our purpose is so important when we set out to do God's work.

In creating divine inspirations at church, one of the most important things to remember is that our churches are not perfect and neither are we. Many times we go to church with our lofty expectations and preconceived notions and then leave disappointed when our expectations are not met. However, the function of the church is not solely to satisfy our individual preferences; the church is the body of Christ and therefore has a calling much greater than any one person within the body, even its leader. We sometimes grow frustrated and resentful toward our church members because they don't behave the way we think they should or because they do or say hurtful things. We can not lose sight of the fact that the church, while set apart from the world, will be an imperfect place because it is filled with imperfect people. We all have hopes of growing stronger in God and developing a closer walk with Him, but we have to remember that God is continuously extending grace and mercy to us. We demonstrate divinity by extending that same grace and mercy to those around us. The best way to cope with the perceived shortcomings of our church families is to accept their imperfection as a truth, thereby releasing the need to have them be anything other than what they are. We also have to make special efforts to love our church members as God loves the church. The Bible gives us special instructions for loving other believers because we have a higher calling on our lives. We must not lose sight of how important it is to love those around us, in spite of what they may do and say.

You have the power to transform your church experience through your attitude and your actions. Changing the way you think about your church will help you grow to a place of gaining a deeper appreciation for the gift of fellowship and a more profound connection with God and humanity. Some of the older Christians may be experiencing a lull in their Christian walks. They may be attending Bible study twice each week, heading up several committees and sitting in their favorite pew every week, but the burning desire to know God and cultivate a stronger walk is no longer there. These people are often going through the religious motions instead of being present in their experiences. Without an alive approach to our spiritual lives, drifting into autopilot is easy to do. Creating divine inspirations is about being purposeful in everything you do and being present and available to the many experiences before you each day. This includes your approach to church. We should be mentally and emotionally prepared before we enter the house of the Lord for worship. What could possibly be a more joyous occasion than meeting with God at the beginning of the week to fellowship, pray, and be fed? In spite of the beauty of holy worship, many of us walk into church looking as if we're headed to work on Monday morning or as if we don't know the marvelous Creator we serve! Our God is so big and so amazing that we should be humbled and happy to go before Him and worship Him. Nothing should be allowed to come between us and our praise, for it is in our praise that the love, peace, provision, joy, and rest we need is released into our lives.

Your church should be a place where you can find rest for your soul, renewal for your mind, and inspiration for your spirit. I believe that there is a place of worship for every Christian who longs for fellowship. It may not always be easy to find, but God loves to see throngs of believers gathering together in His name to strengthen, encourage, and love one another. If you are looking for a church home or a place to study God's Word, pray and ask God to guide you to where you should be. Don't be afraid to ask for referrals from friends and co-workers. You never know who God may use to bring you into the fold. Once you begin assessing church homes, consider the leadership and the structure of the church. Ask yourself how you can improve the church and how the church can improve you. Ask yourself if you believe you can be fed

Divine Inspirations

week after week by the church's appointed leaders. Find out if there are programs in place that are consistent with your spiritual goals and lifestyle such as outreach ministries, singles ministries, or children's church. Visit several times before joining because you may have visited on an "off" Sunday for one reason or another. Above all else, allow God's voice to be your guide in deciding where to settle. And once you commit to membership, don't become a pew warmer. Get connected and get active. Create divine inspirations in your place of worship and watch God do the increase to your efforts.

Chapter 5: Enjoying Divine Relationships

When we seek to discover the best in others, we somehow bring out the best in ourselves. –William Arthur Ward

Relationships are a hot topic of discussion in society today and will probably continue to be so as we continue to evolve and adjust to the changing times. Many standards of the past have been done away with, and in their place have come new ways of interacting, some good and some bad. Because no man is an island, one of the most important skills we can ever develop is how to create and sustain healthy relationships. When we hear the word relationship, we often think of romantic partners, but a relationship is any close connection or dealing with another person. We will use the word "relationship" in this chapter to reference any close connection or dealings with another person, and I will qualify the definition with the word "romantic" when it is necessary to make the distinction. When we broaden our definition of relationship, we can more easily appreciate that all of our relationships need care, not just those that are romantic. Our relationships with others are like plants, and our time, energy, and care are the light, water, and nutrients in the soil. Whether the plant is an acquaintanceship with a co-worker, a friendship with a childhood friend, a relationship with a parent, or a relationship with a romantic partner, they all need similar things to grow and remain stable. Too many of us neglect our relationships and then wonder why we have no friends or why people won't be loyal to us. Relationships are not a ball to be pushed down a hill and allowed to roll on their own. They need our attentive support and nurturing care to develop in healthy and lasting ways.

Throughout this chapter, we'll discuss various types of relationships and the different ways you can create divine inspirations in your relationships. Because our relationships are such an important part of our lives, they deserve our attention. In making efforts to be a better person and to become more emotionally intelligent, you will begin to see more divine elements of your life and relationships revealing themselves. The goal of creating divine inspirations in relationships is to make you more effective in your life's purpose, to keep friction and discord to a minimum, and to open the flood gates of happiness, peace, and love in all of your personal relationships. You should note that the development of healthy relationships is a mutually beneficial process and a gift that keeps on giving. As you begin to grow more kind, more giving, and more understanding, those around you will receive your gifts and want to return those same gifts to you. This begins an ongoing cycle of healthy behavior and facilitates safety in a relationship.

There are several important foundations on which divine relationships are built. We will begin by exploring these elements in order to gain an understanding of what is required of us. We'll move on to discuss various types of problems that arise in relationships and divine ways to cure them. Finally, we'll acknowledge that not all bonds are healthy ones and we'll look at ways to assess whether a relationship should be salvaged or discarded. We'll talk about how to disengage from other people safely and with our hearts and minds in tact.

Service To Others

The first and most important part of creating divine inspirations in relationships is an understanding that your gifts are not your own. God has not placed you on this earth to simply enjoy your own pleasures, fulfill yourself as best you can, and then die. You have been put here because there is some gift inside of you. You may be thinking, "No, Lisa, I'm just a regular person." Understand that this attitude is a consequence of your thinking. If you did not have a profoundly unique purpose, why would God have you here? Think of all of the billions of people in the world. We certainly don't need people here for the sake of having more people, so you must realize that you are here for a reason, whether you know what that reason is or not. In a previous chapter, we discussed discovering purpose. If you are unsure of what your specific purpose is, spend some time praying, meditating, and journaling on what makes you happy, what makes you feel alive, and what your natural talents are. The Bible says that God gives freely to those who ask so if you want to know what your purpose is, ask!

Once you know what that purpose is, you must find ways to extend your gifts and talents to others. Nothing that God has given you is yours to keep. You were created to be a vessel of service to those around you, and as you may have already discovered, there is nothing more powerful than giving of yourself to others. Giving is the key that unlocks the door to abundance in your life. As long as you are selfish and only concerned with yourself, you will be unhappy and you will live in limitation and lack. When you decide to give freely and to commit to finding ways to be of service to others, you will find that each effort is met with a divine assistance to increase its power. You will also see that what you give will always be returned to you in increased measure. This is a universal law that cannot be escaped. God has designed this cosmic law to work on behalf of those who understand that to give is to gain.

Serving others not only results in the return of the blessings we give, it also results in better mental and emotional health for us. With so many distractions and trials in our lives, it is easy to become consumed with our problems and see them as being inescapable and impossible. In being of service to others, paradoxically, we often find answers to our own questions and solutions to our own problems. Serving others helps us to remember that we are not the only ones in the world with problems and that we are connected to humanity and to God. When we reach out to people we can help, we confirm that we are not alone in our own need for support and inspiration. Service to others can help us regain perspective on our lives and develop a deeper appreciation for the immense number of blessings around us. Service is an essential element to happiness.

Service also reconnects us with our own power. It is easy to feel helpless in the face of major life problems, but when we see the power we possess to help others and effect change in their lives, it is much easier to see how much power we have to effect that same change in our own lives. We can see God's hand at work, using us to be a blessing to others. Even when we are at our worst, there is someone we can bless. None of us are useless in our ability to serve. We all struggle with the problems of life, and we all feel overwhelmed from time to time, but we can always find strength and peace in service.

Have you ever had a problem that you pondered very deeply for a long period of time but were not able to solve? You gave up and decided to work on something else and in a moment of what seemed like a miracle, an answer came to you. Those moments are certain proof that God is at work on our behalf when we release the need to be in control and to have everything when we want it and how we want it. Service to others acts in this same way. Oftentimes, our minds are so clouded with the negative aspects of a problem that we can not see the positives of the issue nor can we begin to find a healthy and appropriate way to solve the matter. One of the best things we can do is allow our minds to rest and give ourselves to another task. When we set about helping others, the light we need to see our solutions is often turned on very brightly. The simple act of allowing our subconscious minds to work while our conscious minds rest can result in divine revelations that can give us peace and a new attitude toward our perceived problems. You may have heard of stories of great artists or inventors who have been inspired to get to the next level in their work while doing something completely unrelated like talking with a friend or cleaning the bathroom. Much in the way we can be inspired when we are doing mundane tasks, we can be inspired in a brand new way when we are helping others and allowing ourselves to receive the gifts that are available to us. We do ourselves and everyone else a great service when we take a break from our sorrows and extend ourselves to someone in need.

Love

Many people believe that love is a noun. They associate love with a feeling of butterflies when they are near a certain person or the fact that they think of a person often. However, love extends far beyond society's typical definition. Love is the single most important thing a person of God and a person of divine inspirations can learn to do. Without love, it is impossible to reach a place of completeness as a person. Not only must we love God with all of our hearts, souls, and minds, we must learn to extend love to those around us. We must also learn to love ourselves. Without a healthy love for God and for ourselves, it is difficult, at best, to love others the right way. If love does not live in our hearts and minds, we can not extend it to others. Again, you can not give what you do not have, and in the case of love, any reception of what you do not have will be short-lived, because love feeds off of love. Trying to receive love when you do not have love in your heart is like pouring water into a bottomless container and expecting it to fill up. Your own love – for God, yourself and others – acts as the bottom of your heart that receives loves. As others pour love into your life and your heart, you begin to fill up and eventually overflow with love. This is the optimal place to be as a human being because each act, each touch, and each thought is then colored with love which results in a divine human experience.

Love is so important that the Bible discusses it at length. Jesus constantly reminded his followers how important love was and that He wanted us to love one another. The Bible even offers a working definition of love that gives us an idea of just how important love is and how powerful it is. Let's take a moment to study what love is and how we can achieve the Biblical standard of love in our lives.

1 Corinthians and Romans give clear and tangible definitions and instructions on love. 1 Corinthians 13:4-8a says, *"Love is patient. Love is kind. It does not envy, it does not boast, it is not proud. It is not rude, it is not self-seeking, it is not easily-angered, it keeps no record of wrongs. Love does not delight in evil but rejoices with the truth, It always protects, always trusts, always hopes, always perseveres. Love never fails."* Wow! That's pretty straight-forward, don't you think? I'm sure God's clarity on this issue only reiterates how important love is. Often times, churches disagree over issues that are vague or not specifically outlined in the Bible, but there is no word spared in the discussion of love.

Love is patient

Patience is necessary for love. Notice that patience was the first trait listed in the lineup. I don't believe this was on accident. Have you ever dealt with a person who didn't understand you and she or he became hostile? They had little patience with you and did not make any efforts to understand your needs. This kind of behavior is not a demonstration of love. Patience requires that we allow ourselves to be sympathetic to the needs of those around us, even if that sympathy is not convenient for us. Patience is one of the most important traits we can develop in our growth as people of God. Patience doesn't just involve being patient with other people. We also need to be patient with ourselves and with God. We demonstrate our love and trust for God when we wait patiently for Him to meet our needs and to do what He has promised us He would do. Patience is accepting a difficult situation from God without giving Him a deadline to remove it. And the amazing truth of this is that God's timing is perfect. We never know what unseen dangers He's protecting us from or how He plans to bless us. Impatience can be a huge blessing blocker.

Have you ever been in the middle of a situation and had no clue why something so pointless, difficult and heart-wrenching was happening? Your suffering appeared pointless, senseless, and undeserved. Well, sometimes God uses adversity to mold us and shape us. Of course, gold will never be pure without fire. If we intend to live a divine life, we have to be willing to endure some hardship in order to gain wisdom, understanding, and gratitude. When we grow to love ourselves, we can be patient with ourselves as we transition through the many changes that we will experience throughout our lives. In one of Kirk Franklin's songs, he says, "Some of us wouldn't pray if we didn't go through something." And it's true. When God is raining down His blessings on us, it's easy to get comfortable and start slacking in our prayer lives and our efforts to maintain intimacy with God. But when storms are raging in our lives, we cling to Him. He longs to have that same level of communion with us all the time. We should be in that same perpetual state of praise, thanksgiving, and petition, regardless of what is going on around us. That's why the old folks used to tell us to "stay prayed up" because you never know when you may not be able to pray for yourself.

I have gone through a period of time when I couldn't pray for myself, and to this day, I continue to thank God for my mother and my father because without their intercession, I would probably be dead, and that's no exaggeration. God literally carried me through my storm because I was ready to quit my life.

The funny thing is that sometimes, we look back on our lives and on situations we've dealt with, and we're glad that we had that difficult situation or that season of grief. Have you ever wanted something really badly, not gotten it, and then later been glad that you didn't get it? It's definitely happened to me. God knows what's best for us, and giving Him complete control of our lives lends itself to Him covering us, guiding us, and prospering us. He cultivates patience in our lives by giving us what we need, when we need it and not a second sooner. He is patient with us in spite of us, and He gives generously and graciously.

I'm always saying that faith is the cornerstone of my life, and without it, I would be lost. It's true, especially where patience is concerned. Because truthfully, how can you *truly* be patient and wait on something if you're not even sure that it's coming? When you have no doubts in your mind that God is working on your behalf, that He is your portion, that He loves you unconditionally and wants nothing more than to give you the desires of your heart that are within His will, then it's easy to be patient. The problem is that too many of us are lacking in faith. The Bible says we only need faith the size of a mustard seed! Do you know how small that is? Those things are really small! That should be easy. We only need that much faith to have any and every thing we want according to God's will. The Bible says according to your faith shall it be done unto you so essentially, your blessings, to some degree, will be proportionate with your faith. Some folks can't understand why they can't shake that illness or can't get that job or can't find true love, but they are out of fellowship with God and do not have faith that the things they desire will come to pass. I'm going to let you in on a secret: nothing "unbelievable" or "impossible" is ever going to happen to you. Every single miracle in your life must be believable to you before it will manifest and every single thing you perceive to be "impossible" must become possible in your mind, with patience and faith in God. If you believe that your God specializes in the impossible (mine does) then you should behave that way in speech and in action. That means doing things that reflect your faith and speaking excellence into existence in your life.

Remember to be patient with yourself and with others. Proverbs 19:11 tells us that a man's wisdom gives him patience. Be wise and have patience with those in need, with yourself, and with your loving God who will never fail you.

Divine Inspirations

Love is kind. It does not envy, it does not boast, it is not proud. It is not rude, it is not self-seeking, it is not easily-angered, it keeps no record of wrongs.

Kindness is discussed at length in the Bible. The Bible places tremendous emphasis on interpersonal relations. There is a reason for this. God knew that our relationships would be extremely important to our survival and success in our lives. He knew that without understanding how to effectively relate to each other, we would have a hard time living up to our full potential as human beings.

A working definition of kindness is offered in the verses of 1 Corinthians. It says that love does not envy. Have you ever had a friend who seemed jealous of you and your accomplishments? Oftentimes, that kind of behavior can be the death of what would otherwise be a great friendship. Perhaps this person has a great personality, and you enjoy spending time with them. However, when you share your accomplishments, expecting to hear congratulations and celebration, that person finds ways to discredit what you've done or they immediately begin outlining all of the similar things they've done. This need to "one up" you will probably become so much of a burden at some point that you cease being friends with that person or you stop sharing your accomplishments. The detriment that envy can cause in relationships is why love does not envy. If a person loves you, he or she will not feel the need to marginalize your accomplishments to make themselves feel better. The same is true of boasting. We've all been annoyed at one time or another by the "showboat". In groups we often see situations where a person with low self-esteem feels the need to constantly brag on possessions or accomplishments. Not only does it make that person look insecure, it's usually uncomfortable for those of us who have to listen to the bragging. The Bible mentions this along with the absence of pride because love has the nature of humility. Love seeks to put others before self. When we love ourselves and others, we do not need to lift ourselves up by putting others down nor do we need to make efforts at validating ourselves by boasting.

Love is not rude. Yes, I know this is not the most comfortable topic, but this is not my definition; it's the Bible's. Many of us are guilty of being walking contradictions when it comes to how polite or patient we are with others. We will attend church on Sunday and shout, cry, and wave our hands, but as soon as we get in the car, we're cursing at other drivers on the road or gossiping to friends about what another member at church was wearing. This behavior is completely inconsistent with our walk as Christians! Love is not rude or easily angered. If you find yourself angered by small things, you may need to re-evaluate some things about your walk. God has not called us to respond to life the way the world does. In fact, He has given us specific instruction to be in the world but not of the world. That means we have to make a special effort to purge things in our personalities that are not consistent with the Biblical definition of love. In situations where our patience is tried, we should pause to ask ourselves how we can show love to the person on the receiving end of our actions. We have to remember that God is always watching us. We should behave as we would if God were standing next to us. We also have to remember that we reap what we sow. This fact is a Biblical principle and universal law that cannot be escaped. Because of this, we should be mindful of how we speak to others and how we treat others. If we are rude, unkind, and arrogant towards others, we can rest assured that that same rudeness, unkindness, and arrogance will come back to visit us in one form or another. The Bible makes it clear that God looks at our hearts and the intent of our actions. When we act maliciously, we not only disappoint God, but we also set ourselves up to be on the receiving end of the cosmic boomerang of our actions. In contrast, when we demonstrate love, even to those who are not loving to us, we can maintain a clear conscience and avoid unnecessary strife. When we sow love, respect, and kindness into our lives and into the lives of others, we reap the same. This is much of the reason that giving is such a gift to the giver, not just the receiver. When you extend yourself in love to another person, you can not help but reap some benefit from the exchange, both in the moment and in the future as your blessings to others begin to come back to you multiplied.

Love does not keep a record of wrongs. This is a tough one for many of us because we have not learned what it means to forgive, and our minds have a way of keeping us trapped in the past with our inability to release hurts, resentments, and anger. Some of us are walking around hurt today about things that were said or done years ago. Oftentimes, we are angry with people who have no idea that they've hurt us. In our self-righteousness, we believe that they should "just know" that they've hurt us, and that we are owed an apology and so much more. What we have to remember is that forgiveness is not a gift that we give to our transgressor; it is a healthy choice we make for our own emotional and mental wellbeing. There is no value in staying mad, regardless of who was wrong and who was right. When we love someone, we do not spend time keeping track of their rights and wrongs. Part of being loving is extending mercy to those around us much in the way God extends mercy to us. Think of how many things you've done that have hurt God or disappointed Him. Imagine what kind of shape we would be in if God kept score the way we did! We are not good enough to earn His mercy, and so, we should be mindful of extending that same unfailing mercy to others, whether we consider them worthy or not.

We also have to remember that it is our duty is to forgive. The Bible is clear on that. However, we have to be smart about our post-forgiveness actions. Notice that the Bible does not say that we should allow people to mistreat us. It also does not say that we should go full steam ahead back into a relationship with the person who wronged us. It says that love does not keep a record of wrongs. Some people would liken this to forgetting, but not keeping a mental record of something does not imply that you forget any and every event that has ever happened. Forgiving and reconciling are two separate acts. We must always find ways to forgive, for ourselves and for God. However, our choice to reconcile should be done cautiously and with consideration. We can choose to reconcile with a person who has hurt us and move past the hurtful action. We can also decide that while we have forgiven a person's action(s), it is not wise for us to return to the previous way of operating. Not every person is worthy of our trust so we must be discerning in who we allow into the intimate places of our hearts for they are the wellspring of life. The important thing to remember is that if we do decide to reconcile with that person, we have to be willing to release that person from the perceived debt that they owe us. No one likes to feel like they are in a constant place of working to repair a broken relationship. At some point, the transgressor wants to feel that she or he has re-earned some trust and stability in the relationship. By constantly reminding the transgressor of their actions or holding on to the memory of the action, we do the relationship a disservice, and we make it difficult to move forward.

Love does not delight in evil but rejoices with the truth, It always protects, always trusts, always hopes, always perseveres. Love never fails.

We've all been guilty of celebrating the failure or misfortune of a person who has wronged us. Perhaps we sought revenge on that person or perhaps we hoped that karma would come back to visit them. However, love does not celebrate in such misfortune. As 1 Corinthians points out, love does not delight in evil. We should be mindful that we've all done something wrong to someone at point or another. If we wish to have mercy and forgiveness shown to us, we must extend the same to others. We also must remember that vengeance and the administration of justice belongs to God. When we attempt to get even with people who have wronged us, we do greater harm to ourselves in the long run. God sees all and is able to deal with each of us appropriately. In our anger and frustration, we never know what another person is dealing with. We may never know a person's situation or circumstances that cause them to behave a certain way. Oftentimes, the best course of action we can take is to be still before God and allow His will to prevail.

Not seeking revenge on those who have wronged us does not mean that we should not tell the truth. The verse above says that love rejoices with the truth. We should never be afraid to speak the truth in love and to honestly communicate our feelings. Other people who love and care about us will not take offense to the honest communication of our feelings. In fact, as the verse points out, the person we approach with our feelings should rejoice in the truth as that is the indication of love. Likewise, we should extend that same kindness and love to others. Sometimes, we get offended when people tell us that we've hurt their feelings or done something to offend them. Rather than take this personally or attack that person, we should honestly consider whether our actions or words have harmed that person and whether we were considerate of that. Then we should communicate our appreciation to that person for being honest with us. A person who tells us the truth is a person who is giving us a gift. The truth, even if we don't want to hear it, can help us grow into the best people we can be. The divine life is one that is lived in the truth every day. There is a saying that the truth that has set us free will in the end make us glad also. I love this quote because so often, we don't like the "ugly truth" when we hear it, but in the long run, we can dramatically improve our lives and our relationships if we will rejoice in the truth and allow it to work its transformative work in us.

Love always hopes, trusts, protects, and perseveres. Wow! That's a tall order. As human beings with limited concepts of love, we may be overwhelmed at the thought of love being so many profound things, but with our commitment to truly being loving individuals comes the immeasurable abundance of peace, joy, and abundance that love can yield. Love never fails. Think about that. How many things in our lives never fail? Many of us have things in our lives that we believe are sturdy and dependable. It may be a relationship, a car, or a product. We're convinced that it will always hold up for us, but we've all been disappointed at one point or another by something we expected to last forever. Over time, we learn how to manage disappointment, and we even grow to expect things to last temporarily. We never have to live in anticipation of the failure of love. God has given us the gift of His love, and He has promised to never leave us or forsake us. What a gift! There is no human being who can love us the way God does. Think of all the many things He's forgiven and the many gifts He's given. No matter how much a person may love us or think of us, they simply can not measure up to the ultimate lover of our souls. This is why we must never take our eyes off of God. Our spouses, family members, children, and friends may be wonderful gifts to us, and they may even be tirelessly devoted to us and our causes, but we have to be careful about putting people and things ahead of God. Without an active and healthy relationship with God, we find it difficult to love others the way we should, and our efforts to live up to the Biblical definition of love feel like climbing a mountain. When we allow the love of God to imbue our lives with peace and abundance, we become much more in tune with what it means to love and how to give love each and every day to those we love and those we don't.

Now that we have a working definition of what love is, let's consider some of the problems that arise in relationships and how we can heal the hurts that may come. In our relationships with other people, things happen. One of the most important skills we can learn as adults is how to effectively handle conflict because no relationship will ever be perfect. As we grow and learn how to communicate effectively, how to be more patient and giving, and how to develop emotional intelligence and empathy, we can enjoy more rich and lasting relationships. Every relationship that you have can be enhanced with a stroke of your own brush. If you feel that your relationship with someone has reached a stand still or that a misunderstanding has driven a wedge between you and someone you care about, I guarantee that your actions and attitude can have an effect on the situation. The most important thing for you to do is to decide whether you're prepared to do the work to mend the relationship or free yourself from the limitations that have been set.

Communication

We often hear that communication is the most important thing in a relationship. There is a reason that this is said so often. Communication is the connecting link between two people. Communication is how we connect, form understandings, and create bonds. With great communication, we can enjoy intimacy and safety. With poor communication, we suffer from frustration, anger, and resentment. Without effective communication, the best of intentions mean nothing. Therefore, one of the most important keys to living a divine life is communicating effectively with others.

An important place to start in a discussion on communication is listening. Many of us think that we listen all the time when we are actually psuedolistening. Psuedolistening is what happens when someone is talking to us while we are writing a grocery list or thinking about what we will say next. Obviously, these things are distractions and will prevent us from having a deep understanding of what the other person is saying. Instead, we should be listening actively. Active listening means that we are listening closely to what the person is saying and making a genuine effort to understand the point and intent of the communication. Additionally, when we listen actively, we often ask intelligent questions that check for understanding of what the other person is saying and that further our understanding of what the person is saying. The difference between psuedolistening and active listening can be night and day. It can result in better relationships and an enhanced feeling of connectedness to those around us.

In addition to being great listeners, we have to learn how to effectively express ourselves. Many of us were taught ineffective communication techniques from the time we were small children. We may have learned that when people don't listen to us, we should talk louder. Perhaps, we started a habit of being hostile with people who didn't listen to us. Or maybe we were taught to blame other people for our emotions. These are examples of ineffective communication styles that many adults possess and use on a daily basis. As divinely inspired people, our communication should reflect the excellence that we pursue in other aspects of our lives. Below, I've listed a few tips for effective communication.

> Take opportunities to listen! You may have heard the saying that God gave us two ears and one mouth so that we could listen twice as much as we talk. This is true, and the wisest people I know are excellent listeners. Active listening gives you an opportunity to learn more about the person you're speaking to and about how other people think and operate. When you listen, you are observing and gathering information. The more information you have, the more intelligently you are able to speak and make decisions. When we appreciate that the words out of a person's mouth are a reflection of their beliefs and thoughts, we can deal with them more effectively.

> Always speak respectfully. No one likes to be yelled at or insulted. Be mindful of the tone and volume you use with others. I'm sure you've heard the saying that it's not what you say but how you say it. It's very true! Many times, the translation of words that we hear has more to do with nonverbal cues than with the actual words themselves. Be aware of this as you communicate with

others. Approach people the way you want to be approached. Even when another person is wrong, be careful not to attack or be accusatory with other people. There is a diplomatic and tactful way to say everything so when you are in a situation that warrants confrontation, consider the other person's feelings. Remember that there may be motivations and influences on this person that you are completely unaware of yet are still at play. Whenever I have to deliver unpleasant news or address a conflict, I stop for a moment to think about how I would feel if this person said these words to me. I ask myself how I would want to be approached if I had to hear the news that I'm about to deliver. Doing this has allowed me to behave in much more considerate and loving ways to those around me, even total strangers. Even if someone has done the unthinkable to you, that person is still a human being. Be mindful of that whenever you approach others.

Take responsibility for your emotions. When another person wrongs us, it's easy to blame that person for what we feel and how we respond. This behavior is unproductive and selfish. As adults, we should remember that no one is responsible for our lives but us. When we do not own our thoughts, feelings, and actions, we give our power away to the other person(s) in the situation. The more mature thing to do is to take responsibility for our emotions while still respectfully addressing whatever the person has done or said. This may go something like this, "Karen, I felt brushed off when I called you and you told me you didn't have time to speak with me. I really needed someone to talk to, and I didn't feel you were there for me. I'd like to remain good friends with you, and I hope that I can meet your needs and have you do the same for me." Notice that the word "I" is used often. A less healthy approach would be something like this, "You know, I really hate it when you blow me off. You always do that, and I'm sick of it. You need to stop filling your schedule to the brim so you can have time for your friends. You should learn how to be a better friend." Notice how often "you" is used in the second example. This kind of talk sounds accusatory and places all of the blame and responsibility with the other person. In most situations, the other person is not solely to blame for what we are feeling and neither are we. Offenses, just like acts of kindness, are often a collaborative effort to some degree, and we must stay mindful of that. Remember that your emotions are yours, and that you should own them as such. We hope that those who love us will never hurt us or offend us, but we have to remember that others, like ourselves, are not perfect, and that they deserve to be dealt with fairly and with kindness.

Emotional Intelligence

In the process of learning to listen and communicate effectively, we also have to remember that the foundation all of our efforts should be kindness and patience as mentioned earlier. If we examine God's relationship with us, we see infinite patience, forgiveness, mercy, and love. We are called to extend these same characteristics to those around us. When we do so, we can find healthier ways to manage our expectations of others and build our relationships. One of the best ways to do this is to accept that the people in our lives, even those we love the most, will not be perfect. They will anger, upset, and frustrate us, but that does not mean that those people do not love us. They are simply flawed, just like us. Also, we have to remember that more often than not, those who love us mean well. Sometimes, someone may say something to us in passing or do something without thought that offends us. While we may feel violated, we have to consider that the "offender" may genuinely be innocent and not know any better. If we can take a moment to think about the other person's intent and history with us, we'll often find that the person did not mean any harm and that if we truly feel violated or hurt, we can find a healthy way to address the issue using some of the communication tips discussed above.

We should also develop empathy and emotional intelligence. Many of us do not realize how unaware we are of ourselves and others in an emotional sense. We may go about our day completely oblivious to how what we do and say affects others. One of the most precious gifts we can give to those we love is consideration of their feelings. Too often, we are completely absorbed in our own lives and our own feelings without considering the tremendous effect we may have on others. This could be as simple as addressing a grocery clerk by name or as profound as knowing how to comfort a friend who has just lost a loved one. What I've found is that my efforts to reach out in kindness and love are often reciprocated. However, I had to learn how to tailor my efforts along the way. What I realized is that we all have different love languages and that we all want to be loved in unique ways. I've learned that while an act of love to one person may be giving them a copy of their favorite book on CD, that may not mean much to another person. To one person, bringing food to them while they are ill may mean the world while another person may value having their space and time respected while they are not well. Our experiences, preferences, and circumstances are all different and have a critical effect on how we want to be approached and handled. If we can stay mindful of this, we can be more successful in relating to those around us. In the process of attempting to understand others and sympathize with them, we must also allow others to do the same for us. Throughout our lives, we will find people who come into our lives for various reasons, and we will find that there are people who genuinely care about us and want to reach out to us. Rather than being on the defensive, we should learn to both think critically about the situation and also lovingly accept the things they want to offer to us. Once we have developed healthy and safe relationships, we can feel confident calling on the people closest to us when we need them.

When we are going through a difficult time, we may hesitate to call even our family members or friends because we don't want to burden them with our troubles. We may feel that talking with others in an honest way may be an inconvenience to them. This can be especially true if we've been going through a series of challenges or a long-term trial, and our stories and complaints repeat themselves. What we should remember is that this is when our friends can fulfill their potential in our relationships. True friends who care deeply about us do not want to see us suffer. They want to help us, listen to us, and comfort us, even if the process is one that is ongoing. If we are self-conscious about reaching out, we can check with them to make sure it's a good time for them before we start talking or we can be sure that they are in the proper state of mind to assist us. If we find that we have reached that friend at a bad time, we can call back at another time, or call another friend.

Think about how you would feel if your very best friend or closest family member was in a tremendous amount of pain and you knew nothing of it. What if this same person was dealing with a problem that you could help solve, but because you knew nothing of it, that person had to suffer in silence? I find that thought unsettling because I don't like the concept of human suffering, but I certainly don't like the idea of someone close to me suffering needlessly. What we have to remember is that our friends want to be there for us the way we want others to allow us to be there for them. We want them to call us and share their sorrows with us, as well as their joys, because this is how we develop our friendships and share our lives. If you cannot call on your friends at your lowest point, then when can you? If your friends are only there for you when you are happy and celebrating and then disappear when hardship is upon you, you may need to reconsider those people as friends. A true friend will not abandon you when you need that person the most. If you are feeling self-conscious about having a tough time, you can bring this fact into the conversation by acknowledging it and giving that person an opportunity to address your insecurity. Chances are your friend will reassure you that he or she has no problem with being there for you and is happy to do so. We can share how that person can best help us, whether it be through empathetic listening or offering insight on the situation.

Without our friends and family, we would be hard pressed to get through the tough times and celebrate the good ones. Again, none of us are islands, and we all need someone in this life. When we learn to depend on those around us in healthy ways, we can forge deep bonds and have our needs meet. If we leave our friends out of our processes when the going gets tough, our friendships can begin to feel superficial and flighty. When we include our friends in the full story of our lives—the good, the bad, and the ugly—we can build profound and authentic relationships in which we are free to be who we are and allow others to be the same. When we do this, we invite our friends to bring their whole selves to the relationship as well which results in a beautiful and safe connection for love to flourish.

As we all know, relationships do not always end well. As I mentioned earlier, some people will come into our lives for a season or a reason while others will come to stay. We do not always know right away why someone has come into our lives, but if we will remain prayerful and present, the purpose of our relationships is often revealed to us. Nevertheless, disconnecting with a loved one is difficult. This could include the end of a long friendship or a difficult divorce. We never know where life will take us, but we do have control over how we respond to the things that happen to us.

Like the act of marriage that binds two people together, separation is the result of a life-altering decision. It is the dissolving of a relationship that we believed would last our whole lives. We may not even be able to articulate how we got to this place, yet we may also feel we have no choice but to sever this tie. Whatever we feel, we need the support of the friends and family who will stand by us no matter what we decide. At some point, we may need to be challenged to look deeper inside ourselves as we make this very important decision, but what we need most of all is unconditional love and loyalty.

Divorce and breakups are processes that, once in motion, become difficult to stop, and this can be painful if we find ourselves having second thoughts. We may feel that we should do more to save the marriage, or we may wonder if there is something about ourselves that we could fix or change instead of going through with this painful separation. On the other hand, we may be seeing in hindsight that our relationship was truly only meant to last for a short time so that we could learn something we needed to know. Whatever the case, we need friends who will allow us to linger in confusion when we don't have the answers and who will support us whether we find ways to reconcile and stay in the relationship or whether we walk away.

Of course, the most essential Ally we have lives inside our hearts and speaks to us from within. God will always order our steps if we humbly submit our will to His and commit to being obedient. We can trust God to send the Holy Spirit to comfort us and to send people who will support us in kind and loving ways as we navigate the rough terrain of confusion and loss. Sometimes all we can do is look to the horizon,

Divine Inspirations

remembering that we will get through this time, and no matter what happens we will once again feel whole.

One of the hardest decisions we ever make in life is leaving a long-term relationship that just isn't working. When attempts at repairing and working out issues are not effective, it may be time to examine moving on. I firmly believe that most relationships can be mended if more people would look at them differently and selflessly. In spite of that belief, I realize that there are times when the union of two people is much more toxic than their separate existence. We are emotional creatures, and when our heartstrings are tied to those of another, separating from that person can feel like something inside of us is being ripped in an extremely painful way. It is not something most of us will take lightly, and many of us will struggle with our desire to stay in a relationship that is unfulfilling simply in order to avoid that pain. We may question whether the happiness we seek even exists, and we may wonder if we might be wiser to simply settle where we are, making the best of what we have. On the one hand, we almost relish the idea that true happiness is not out there so that we can avoid the pain of change. On the other hand, we feel within ourselves a yearning to fulfill our desire for relationships that are vital and healing. God intended for our relationships to fulfill us and draw us closer to Him. Many of us know that there is a calling for us to have more. Ultimately, most of us will follow this call, because deep within ourselves we know that we deserve to be happy and that God does not intend for relationships to destruct us and draw us from Him. We all deserve to be respected and cherished, no matter where we find ourselves in this moment, and we are all justified in moving, like plants toward the light, in the direction that leads to our greatest fulfillment. First, though, we should seek God and His opinion on our actions. If we are in His will, He will grant us the strength and courage to move on from the relationship that appears to be holding us back.

Taking the first step is hard, but the peace we find when we have freed ourselves from a situation that is draining our energy will outshine any hardship we undergo to get there. If we remember that this too shall pass, we can begin the work of disentangling ourselves from the relationship that no longer fits. Every step brings us closer to a relationship that will work and the freedom we need to find the happiness we deserve.

Overcoming Heartbreak

No discussion of relationships would be complete without some mention of overcoming heartbreak. Almost all of us have had our hearts broken at one time or another, and we are all affected in different ways. Some of us are able to recover quickly and valiantly while others of us wallow in self-pity and writhe in the agony of a broken heart. There are some important things to remember when we are facing heartache. I consider heartbreak to be a very serious matter because it is capable of driving us to behave in unhealthy ways. I realize that sometimes, the sheer size of the emotions we face in the midst of a difficult breakup can be enough to destroy even the best of us. Sometimes the habits we form when soothing our wounds become crutches and hindrances on our paths to recovery and redemption.

The first and most important thing we must do when we feel that our lives are spinning out of control is to remember who is in control. Although we may feel helpless and hopeless, we have to remain mindful of the fact that God has not left us. He loves us dearly and wants what's best for us. The Bible tells us that God is close to the brokenhearted. Although we are not promised a life free from pain or disappointment, God has promised to send the Holy Spirit to us to comfort us and be with us in our times of need. All we have to do is ask for God's assistance to overcome our challenges.

Second, we must choose recovery. You may have heard the saying from Abraham Lincoln, "Most folks are about as happy as they make their minds up to be." I subscribe to this belief, especially when it comes to an aching heart. Sometimes it is next to impossible to see the silver lining on the clouds of doubt that invade our world when we're nursing a broken heart, but we can not act soberly and rationally if we have not yet committed to recovery. If you are facing heartache, choose recovery. That means that you can see yourself on the other side of your heart break – healed, happy, and completely free of the burden of the relationship gone awry. Without a conscious choice of recovery, getting better and feeling better will feel like an overwhelming uphill battle. The road to brighter days will be difficult enough without waffling about whether to really get out there and do things that will help move the healing process along.

Once we commit to getting better, we have to consider the resources available to us to help us move past the pain. This could include things like exercising, taking a class, spending more time with friends and family, and other goals that were put off during the relationship. Exercise has actually been shown to help treat depression so I very highly recommend regular exercise as a part of a personal therapy regimen for overcoming heartbreak. Setting and achieving goals is another important tool for feeling good again. This could include developing a hobby or doing volunteer work. Perhaps there's a foreign language you've always wanted to learn or some redecorating that you want to do. A brainstorming session should help you come up with some constructive ways to get better and develop yourself at the same time.

Remember that your friends and family are great to lean on during a difficult time. As we discussed earlier in the chapter, these people are there to act as a support system and to help you retain some sense of familiarity and comfort with your life as you know it. Some people tend to withdraw from those closest to them when they face a trial, but the best thing we can do is turn to those who love us and want to help us through our pain. Not only can we help ourselves by allowing others to put the balm of listening and love on our wounds, we can also develop deeper bonds with those people by being vulnerable enough to share the most sensitive and sacred of our emotions.

The third thing to remember is that healing is not a linear process. Many books and relationship experts throw out tips like not talking to the person for 30 days or writing a letter and burning it. These things are usually helpful, but time is still the key to healing. There is no way around the healing process, and when we attempt to ignore or rush the process, we usually do more damage than good. The best thing we can do is take the process one day at a time. It's okay to grieve, feel sad, and even feel anger. The important thing is to not allow these emotions to suffocate us and render us unavailable to God and to our lives.

As you move forward in life and make decisions about friends, lovers, and acquaintances, remember what the Bible has to say about love and remember that the only love you keep is the love you give away. Don't forget to forgive whenever you can and to be patient with those you encounter. Remember that when you treat people as if they are what they ought to be, you help them become what they should be.

Chapter 6: Sustaining A Divine Life

First we make our habits, then our habits make us. –Charles C. Noble

Now that we've discussed the various components of a divine life and how we can go about pursuing a divine life, let's look at the long term ideas. When we set out to make changes in our lives, it's easy to change in the short term, but sometimes, we find it more difficult to sustain change over time without reverting to our old ways of doing things. In this chapter, I'll outline some of the keys to sustaining a divine life and important things to remember as you continue on your divine journey.

As we go through life, we'll experience ups and downs. We'll have good days and bad days, but if we look closely at the gifts and opportunities before us, we will see that God is exceedingly merciful to us and gives us new things to celebrate every day. In order to completely appreciate a divine life, we have to see the world around us through a different set of goggles. We have to be able to understand and appreciate that life is indeed good and that happiness is a choice that we make every single day. Many of us believe that our circumstances are responsible for our unhappiness, but the truth is that we are choosing unhappiness. Have you ever met a person in dire straights that had a smile on his or her face? Or have you met a dying cancer patient who seems completely content and peaceful? These types of situations are examples of people who are able to retain their joy in spite of what may be going on around them. The important lesson we can learn from them is that we are all blessed and have things to be grateful for at every point in our lives. Gratitude is the key to abundance. We'll discuss gratitude a little more later in this chapter.

Daily Commitment

The first and perhaps most important aspect to sustaining a divine life is realizing that it is an ongoing process. Because none of us are perfect, we have to afford ourselves room to fail and grow. After all, failure yields tremendous opportunities to grow and develop our character. Think about the times you've attempted something and succeeded with ease the first time versus a time you've attempted something and perhaps failed miserably or tried several times and finally got it right. If you look closely at your failures, you will see open doors for you to learn more about yourself as a person and to grow as a person. Furthermore, you will see that your failures contributed to your successes, even in unrelated aspects of life. Our failures exist to serve purposes in our lives, and when we approach them with this attitude, we can press on with a spirit of gratitude, resolution, and hope.

Several months before I finished this book, I began doing some really important things that changed my life for the better. I decided that I wanted more. Even though my life was moving forward, and I was generally very happy, I felt that I needed a more quantitative way to approach my daily happiness. So, I sat down one day and spent some time really meditating on my best days. I considered the uneventful best days, meaning the days that were "normal" versus the days that were momentous such as births, graduations, accomplishments, etc. As I considered my best days and best seasons, I noticed some common threads in them. I quickly realized that there were several choices I made during those times that resulted in a heightened level of happiness and gratitude for the things I had in my life. During those times, I felt intuitively connected to God and to my higher self. I spent a few months doing trial and error to really narrow down the things that made a significant difference and the things that didn't. What you will read below is the result of that trial and error and is my personal prescription for the development of self-esteem, happiness, and a divine life.

The first thing is committing to my gratitude journal. A gratitude journal is a place where a person can list or write freely about the things she or he is grateful for. I started my gratitude journal because I was too engrossed in the cares and trials of my life. I was complaining often, and I had even started to grow resentful and angry with God. I knew it was time for a change, and I slowly started to realize that gratitude was essential to my happiness. I also knew subconsciously that until I learned to be grateful for the infinite number of blessings I had, I would never be able to unlock the door to abundance in my life.

In the past, I've been less disciplined with my gratitude journaling. I was consistent when it came to journaling about other things, but I needed to buckle down and do the gratitude journaling daily. Once I was consistent, the floodgates flew open, and I had more and more to be grateful for. When we truly learn to develop and cultivate an "attitude of gratitude", we will always have more to be grateful for, and we often see more abundance flowing into our lives. If you don't understand the power of gratitude, you may consider this frivolous or a waste of time, but if you are in any way connected enough to God to understand the importance of remaining grateful, you will completely appreciate the importance of this exercise.

There are many ways to approach gratitude journaling. Some people like to do it by the week while others like to do it daily. Some do it in the morning and some at night. The important thing is that you develop a habit of journaling your gratitude. I have a trusty little notebook that I keep in my handbag, and I use this book as one of my gratitude journals. I like to keep it with me because sometimes I'll have a grateful thought during the day while I'm away from home or maybe some revelation will come to me. I also have a beautifully decorated notebook at home that I journal in daily. The process of gratitude journaling does not have to be long or complicated; it usually takes less than 5 minutes. I split the page in half by writing a line down the middle and I make 2 lists: one list is of 10 things I'm grateful for that day. The other list is of 10 things I believe will come to me, including achievements, people, things, and more. These lists achieve several goals. They help me to contemplate the blessings I receive each day – from the grandiose and big things to the small and mundane things. The gratitude list also helps me to say that every single day, no matter how "good" or "bad" I thought the day was, there is something to be grateful for. The list of hope and faith helps me to stay focused on my goals, and it also acts as a motivator by tying my emotions and prayers to the things I want in my life. Both lists, when done consistently, are very powerful and have affected my life in wonderful ways.

Divine Inspirations

Another amazing daily exercise that has set my life on fire is doing what I call the Big Six every day. The Big Six are six important things that can help transform your life into one that is abundant, happy, and productive. I noticed that I was not feeling as "filled up" about my life as I wanted to, but I didn't entirely understand why. I prayed about the matter and realized that there are certain things in life that are good for us and that over time, those things yield good feelings. I realized that if I were to commit to doing these things daily, my life would begin to look very different over a short period of time.

This list of things must be done every day, even if you have to scramble a little bit to get them in at the end of the day. I personally guarantee that if you will do these six things every day, your life will improve. No ifs ands or buts about it – you will become a better person, your life will be better than before, and those around you will benefit even more from your existence. If you are wrestling with self-doubt, it will improve. If you are battling depression, it will improve. If you feel disconnected from God, it will improve. If you are just plain ol' unhappy, you'll feel better. If you are not achieving your goals or you need to discover what makes you happy, this will help.

1. *Pray.* This is simple yet powerful. Not a single day should pass in which you do not spend time alone in communication with your Creator. I think this is essential to the grounded, centered person who has peace and joy. There is something special about having alone time with God and being able to share our deepest thoughts and feelings with him. Imagine a friend with whom you can be completely free and uninhibited. Consider One whom you can share every detail with and who loves you in a tender, unconditional way. Why would you want to skip such a precious time? God enjoys communion with us, and He can use prayer time to strengthen and encourage us as well as reveal Himself to us. The person seeking to grow as a human being can not afford to forgo the opportunity to plug into such a powerful source. Don't neglect the opportunity to say thank you for all that you have been blessed with and to petition God for those things you desire.

2. *Do something to help someone.* Reaching out to others is good for the human spirit. When we give to others, we not only help others but

also help ourselves. It is impossible for us to give of ourselves and our resources without receiving. The Bible points this out in telling us that we reap what we sow. The act of helping or giving could be something as simple as giving someone directions or giving someone ride. Or it could be a larger commitment like helping a friend write a business plan or committing to cleaning your mom's basement. Either way, we can rest assured that when we make a sincere effort to help others, we will reap the benefits of what we've given many times over. Additionally, helping others will contribute to our self-esteem and mental well-being. It's tough to help someone in need and not feel good for having made someone's life easier and better.

3. *Do something that makes you happy.* Of course, happiness is completely subjective so you'll have to spend time thinking about the things that truly make you happy. This exercise is great because it requires that you think about the things that bring you joy and how you can find little ways to infuse your day with happiness. Doing this exercise has really helped me reconnect with certain aspects of myself that were repressed. You deserve to be happy! You deserve to be happy now…not when you move or make more money or get married or get that promotion or have kids that are well-behaved or lose weight – you deserve it right now! Your happiness act for the day could be short and sweet like a crossword puzzle or something bigger like spending the entire day at the beach (my personal favorite). Regardless, it has to be something completely self-indulgent that totally puts you in a state of bliss, if only temporarily. I have to qualify this by saying that drugs, alcohol, and any type of self-destructive behavior does not fall into this category. You don't want to suffer negative side-effects later from your "happy" act of the day. Be sure that the action edifies you instead of tearing you down.

4. *Do something that makes you a better person.* This also varies from person to person. It could be prayer, journaling, meditating, exercising, reading, or seeing a therapist. For me, it's usually something educational. I typically read 1-3 books every month, and I have found that doing so has been instrumental in my personal development. I've learned about a variety of topics, and I have been able to press forward towards my goals with more knowledge of the world around me. However, the thing that another person chooses that makes him or her a better person may be

very different from mine. The important thing is that you walk away from this act feeling like you've honored your spirit as an individual and that you are better, if only by a small increment, than you were yesterday. You eat an elephant one bite at a time, and you become a bigger, better person one act at a time.

5. *Do something that moves you closer to attaining an important goal.* I can not stress this enough. If you are suffering from feelings of hopelessness or feeling like your life is going nowhere fast, this should be the first thing you do each day. This is important to your growth as a person and to your confidence. The important goal could be losing weight, studying for an important exam, completing a project for work, or preparing a house to be sold. Whatever the goal is, we often feel much happier and more relaxed if we do something – anything – to work towards achieving the goal. Baby steps count on the way to achievement. Remember that even the loftiest of ambitions must be broken up into manageable pieces that can be completed day by day. With an ongoing commitment to doing at least one thing every day that moves you closer to an important goal, you will soon look up and find that you've accomplished a lot and that your goal is much closer than before. Committing to doing at least one thing that moves you closer to one or several of your goals will lead to less fear, less self-doubt, and more confidence. It will also help you stay connected to your purpose and to your personal achievements.

6. *Get moving.* Contrary to how some people live, our bodies were not designed to be sedentary and stagnant. When we consider the complexities of the human body, it is clear that God was not sparing any details when He created us. We have not been given these amazing temples in order to sit around and do nothing. Our bodies function best when we move them every day. This could include strenuous activity like running 5 miles or something simpler like gardening or walking the dog. Either way, the important thing is that we move every day. Studies have shown that movement and exercise are effective at treating depression. The state of our bodies is connected to our emotional and mental well-being and vice versa. When we are able to think positively and live well, our bodies are healthier, and we are less likely to become ill. Likewise, when our bodies are healthy and fit, we tend to feel better about ourselves and about life, and we are more productive. This makes

exercising and recreational activities a win-win situation. Be sure to get up and get moving for at least 30 minutes every day.

Now that we've discussed the benefits of gratitude journaling and the Big Six, let's continue with some other ideas about other things that can help us sustain a divine life. One of the keys to sustaining a divine life is to define happiness so that we can choose it consistently. To begin, let's analyze happiness and how we can mold our attitudes to yield happiness every day.

Analyze Happiness

Those of us on the path of personal and spiritual growth have a tendency to analyze our unhappiness in order to find the causes and make improvements. However, one of the most effective techniques for sustaining a divine life is analyzing our happiness. Since we have the ability to rise above and observe our emotions, we can recognize when we are feeling joyful and content. Then we can harness the power of the moment by savoring our feelings and taking time to be grateful for them. In order to make the most of this analysis, we must make it a point to be present from moment to moment in our lives. We have to remember that while setting goals and looking ahead is important, remaining present and aware of where we are at any given moment is powerful and can help us grow more fulfilled and joyful by being conscious of the abundance surrounding us.

As you may have heard, recognition is the first step in creating change, therefore recognizing what it feels like to be happy is the first step toward sustaining happiness in our lives. Addicts are told that the first step to recovery is admitting that there is a problem. I submit that the first step to happiness is admitting that we can choose to be happy. We can examine how joy feels in our bodies and what thoughts run through our minds in times when we are happy and content. Without diminishing its power, we can reflect on what may have put us in this frame of mind, and then we can take note of the choices we made while there. We might realize that we are generally more giving and forgiving when there's a smile on our faces, or that we are happiest when we are spending time with our families. Whatever the case may be, simply being aware of this can give us insights on what is most important to us and how to invite more happiness into our lives.

Once we know what it feels like and can identify some of our happiness indicators, we can recreate that happiness when we are feeling low. I realized last year that for me, reading something positive and affirming helps to restore my happiness and peace of mind if I have slipped into a bad mood. As we go about sustaining divine lives, we will meet with some challenges and adversity. Knowing that like attracts like, we can pull ourselves out of a bad mood by focusing on joy, peace, and gratitude. We might find that forcing ourselves to be giving and forgiving, even when it doesn't feel good, helps us to reconnect with the joy that usually precedes it. If we can identify simple things in our lives that can help us re-center, we can use them as tools to recapture joy if we are having trouble finding it. By focusing our energy on analyzing happiness and all that it encompasses, we feed, nurture, and attract more of it into our lives, eventually making a habit of happiness.

Growing pains

Maintaining a positive attitude and a measure of faith can be challenging when you are in the midst of difficult times. This is partly because we tend to think that if the God loves us, He will express that by only allowing positive circumstances into our lives. However, we are like children, and God is our infinitely wise and loving Father who knows what our souls need to thrive better than we do. Just as a young child does not benefit from getting everything she or he wants, we also benefit from times of constriction and difficulty to help us grow and learn. The Bible even tells us that God disciplines those He loves and calls His children as an earthly parent does. If we keep our minds stayed on God's unconditional and unfailing love, we can always trust that we are loved even when things are hard.

At the same time, if you truly feel that nothing is going right for you, it's never a bad idea to ask for God's revelation, examine your life and see if there are some changes you can make to alleviate some of the difficulty. Gently and compassionately exploring the areas causing the most trouble may reveal things you are holding on to and need to release such as unhealthy relationships, unprocessed emotions, unresolved transitions, or negative ways of looking at yourself or your life. As you take responsibility for the things you can change, you can more easily surrender to the things you can't, remembering all the while that every phase of your life will, without doubt, give way to another.

One of the most important things to remember in sustaining a divine life is that no negative event or circumstance can permanently destroy or cripple us unless we allow it to do so. Too many people live their lives and govern themselves according to the circumstances that surround them. We must remind ourselves that "this too shall pass" and that God has not left us, even in our darkest hours. We also have to grow to a place of accepting what is. Many of the struggles that we face in life are issues of a lack of acceptance rather than whatever the perceived problem may be. We often blame our lives, other people, or even God for not being where we want to be, not having what we want and not being able to create the lives we desire most for ourselves. It is important to remember that the present moment has been given to us as a gift; it is all we have. Lamenting the past and fearing the future do not serve us on our path to self-actualization. God, in all of His omnipotent glory, is error free. Our small minds can not possibly begin to truly understand His ways. The Bible tells us that His ways are as far from our ways as the east is from the west! That's a long way. His wisdom is infinite, and as we begin to truly appreciate each moment and situation presented to us, we can rest in knowing that God has it all under control. When we learn to accept our lives and our circumstances, we can unlock new truths that empower us and put us on a path to living well.

Getting Comfortable With Discomfort

There are certain things that we must learn to be comfortable with if we are to remain in alignment with the goals of living a divine life. Those things include uncertainty, change, bad days, and failure. We'll examine these things closer in the following paragraphs.

Most folks don't like change. Anything that disturbs the status quo and removes us from our comfort zones is usually not well received. What we must remember is that there is no such thing as a true comfort zone.

Divine Inspirations

The only certain things in our lives are change and God. If we can learn to trust God to be all of the certainty we need, we can be free from the fear of not having enough, not being good enough, and not knowing what is to come.

Change, like uncertainty, is something we simply can not control. The more we attempt to resist necessary changes, the greater the disservice we do to ourselves. We often exert unnecessary energy trying to fight the inevitable instead of appreciating that change can be transformative and can help us grow. Our lives are meant to be a journey; without change, there is no journey. We can not truly discover the deepest parts of ourselves until we are faced with change, particularly unexpected change. Showing up for our lives every day and living truthfully require that we accept life as it is presented to us and allow change to be an ally on our path towards achievement and joy. Those who are able to use change to their advantage are often more successful, happier, and better adjusted in their lives. We can learn from these people by observing that they have learned to consistently make lemonade out of lemons. Along with learning to accept change, we have to develop the ability to persevere through hardships. Many of us never realize the goals and dreams we set for ourselves because we allow ourselves to be easily swayed and deterred by obstacles. The important thing to remember is that God will not bring us to anything that He will not bring us through. He has given us each special gifts to help make this world a better place for those who live in it. Hardships and challenges are a sign that we are attempting to do something worth while. The more we learn to continue on our paths in spite of the circumstances that present themselves, we will find achievement easier.

Another key component to sustaining a divine life is overcoming self-doubt. At some point in our lives there may come a time when we feel insecure about ourselves. We might judge our ability to do something or feel self-conscious about the way we look. It does not matter how this feeling manifests, but it is important to be aware of our thoughts and how they impact our view of ourselves. Once we remember that insecurities are a normal part of life for everyone—even those who appear to be extremely confident—we may find it easier to step back from the uncertainty that lies within and take a more realistic look at ourselves.

The desire to improve or better ourselves is a natural response that arises when we begin to compare our lives to those of other people. It might seem, for example, that we do not have nearly as much going for us as our neighbor, best friend, or coworker. In truth, what we think we see about another person is usually what they want us to notice. They may be putting on a mask, trying to make things in their lives seem better than they are. If we were to look at their lives a little more closely, we would also realize that they are human, full of glorious imperfections that make them who they are. Recognizing this may take some time at first. Should we feel our insecurities begin to surface, taking deep breaths while at the same time acknowledging each one of our gifts will help us become more centered. Doing this allows us to see the wonders that lie within and lets our inner beauty shine forth into the world all the more brightly. When we hold up a detailed mirror to our lives and weigh ourselves against others, we are not able to see the things that make us truly unique. Giving ourselves permission to appreciate all the gifts God has given us, however, will make us feel more secure about ourselves and more able to use our gifts to their fullest.

As I mentioned in the section on the Big Six, gratitude is perhaps the single most important element in maintaining a divine life. Without gratitude, we can not truly develop a deep relationship with God nor can we develop and maintain true relationships with other people. The more we show gratitude, the more we have to be grateful for! Gratitude is truly the key that unlocks the door to abundance in our lives. Think about how you feel when you give someone a gift, and the person fails to say thank you. Even if you didn't give the gift to receive praise or thanks, you may feel slighted or feel that the recipient was ungrateful if they didn't bother to say thank you. Well, how do you think God feels? He is infinitely generous to us and yet so often, we don't thank Him for the many things He does for us. We behave like spoiled children who always have their hands out wanting more, never being conscious or grateful for what we have been given. It is easy to get busy with our lives and forget to appreciate the simple things in life. I went through a period where I didn't realize just how blessed I was until I had some things taken away from me. What I realized was that I was indeed blessed and that I needed to cultivate an attitude of gratitude within myself. I slowly but surely started to understand that we can not wait for the right circumstances or anything outside of us to be grateful.

Bad Days

Have you ever had a day that seemed doomed from the time you got out of bed? We all have days when it feels like the world is against us or that the chaos we are experiencing will never end. One negative circumstance seems to lead to another, and we start to lose hope that the cycle will stop. You may wonder, on a bad day, whether anything in your life will ever go right again or if that day is the beginning of a downward spiral of your life. We must remember that a bad day, like any other day, can be a gift. On our path of divine inspiration, we will meet with bad days. Having a bad day can give us an opportunity to listen to our lives and get in tune with ourselves on a deeper level. A bad day may show you that it is time to slow down, change course, or lighten up. Sometimes we go out about the day with a white knuckle grip on everything that is happening. When we release the need to have everything be how we believe it should, we can more easily adapt to unfavorable circumstances that may arise. A bad day can help you glean wisdom you might otherwise have overlooked or discounted. Bad days can certainly cause you to experience uncomfortable feelings you would prefer to avoid, yet a bad day may also give you a potent means to learn about yourself. Your attitude can make all the difference in whether a bad day is a day of learning or a day of emotional tailspin.

You may consider a bad day to be one where you have missed an important meeting because your car stalled or your computer shut down or you received a piece of very bad news earlier in the morning. Multiple misfortunes that take place, one after the other, can leave us feeling vulnerable and intensely cognizant of our fragility. However, bad days can only have a long-term negative effect on us if we let them. You can reclaim your power and gain control by asking yourself what you can learn from these kinds of days. Make it a point to see "problems" as challenges and opportunities to learn and grow. In doing so, you are able to quickly turn a bad day into a great day by virtue of having learned an important lesson, developed your character, or increased your self-esteem.

Bad days contribute to the people we become. Though we may feel discouraged and distressed on our bad days, a bad day can teach us patience and perseverance. It is important to remember that your attitude drives your destiny and that one negative experience does not have to be the beginning of an ongoing stroke of bad luck. A bad day is memorable because it is one day among many good days. Otherwise, we would not even bother to acknowledge it as a bad day. Remember that everybody has bad days. Reach out to your friends and loved ones if you need advice or a listening ear. You are not alone, and the world is not against you. After all, if God is for you, who could possibly be against you? Each day is a new gift, and with God on our sides and a great attitude in our minds, we can face each day with peace, purpose, and divine inspiration.

Chapter 7: A Call To Action

To accomplish great things, we must not only act, but also dream; not only plan, but also believe. –Anatole France

Here we are at the end of our brief time together. What will you do now? The concepts in this book may have been a review for you or perhaps this information is new to you. Either way, you owe it to yourself and to the world around you to use this information in a constructive and positive way.

As you go forward, remember that God loves you dearly. He wants the very best for you, and because you were created in His image, you are a creator. You have the power to shape the world around you. Your inner world creates your outer world. The unique gifts and talents you have been given are your gifts to the world. Be a giver! There are choices and actions that will lead you in different directions, and it is through those choices and actions that you create your realities. Sometimes we choose to do something that takes us in the opposite direction of the reality we want to create for ourselves. When we do this, we feel bad—uneasy, unhappy, unsure. We might go so far as to label ourselves "bad" when a situation like this arises. Instead of labeling ourselves, though, we can simply acknowledge that we made a choice that lead us down a particular path, and then let it go, forgiving ourselves and preparing for our next opportunity to choose to act in ways that support our best intentions. Be conscious of who you are and who you are becoming. Don't allow your life and anything in it to be an accident. You posses the power to do great things. The very seeds of greatness are planted deep within your soul. With proper care, those seeds can grow into massive talents and blessings that will ultimately catapult you into self-actualization and an inspired life.

You are a human being with every right to be here, learning and exploring and growing. To label yourself good or bad is to think too small. What you are is a decision-maker and every moment provides you the opportunity to move in the direction of your higher self or in the direction of degradation. In the end, only you know the difference. Remember to live by God's standards and your standards; no one else's matter. If you find yourself going to a place of self-judgment, try to stop yourself as soon as you can and come back to center. Know that you are not good or bad, you are simply you. Embrace yourself; embrace the complexities that make you who you are. To do anything less is to insult God's flawless design. Remember that you have the power to be the solution to every perceived problem and to create the love, joy, peace, and abundance you deserve in your life.

Go forward and live well. Live the life of your dreams. Don't wait until "when" to begin; start today. You are not promised anything but the present, and you must milk every moment for all it's worth. The first step to getting what you want in life is knowing what you want. This may sound obvious, but a surprising number of us are going through life without really coming to terms with the truth of what we want. There are many reasons for this, and they range from influences that curb our imaginations to external factors that curb our ability to take action. We may feel that getting too caught up in exploring our deepest desires is wasted energy when it seems we want things beyond our grasp. This is a very practical attitude and has its benefits, but it can be safely balanced with a more imaginative and unlimited approach to the question of what we want. We may feel unbalanced when we take a step, but when we allow our souls to be anchored in God and in the truth of ourselves, we can assuredly move to new heights.

Remember that butterflies can't see their wings. In spite of how beautiful their wings are, and in spite of how important wings are to a butterfly's survival, the butterfly can not see the wings; it can only feel them. And so it is with you and your faith. You may not be able to see how God will use you or how your path will unfold, but if you trust God, you will be able to feel yourself gracefully fluttering through life and enjoying the environment. If the butterfly only believed what it could see, it would never fly, and its experience would be limited to the ground. I challenge you to trust that your wings are there and that they are beautiful. People admire your design and your metamorphosis. Your very existence is a testament to God's handiwork. Live your life as an adventure of evolution and purpose.

If you take nothing else away from this book, take away the love of God and the power that lies in you to be, do, and have divine inspirations.

God bless you.

A Special Invitation

I absolutely love connecting with people, including my readers and fans. I have had the experience of e-mailing an author after completing his or her book and never getting a response or getting a generic, form letter.

With that in mind, I am extending an invitation to you to be in touch. My company, Life With Inspiration, is designing a wide range of products and services designed to help you take your life to the next level. As the name suggests, we teach people to live life with inspiration. Our personal development division, Rich In Spirit, takes a holistic approach to life management. In the coming year, I will be conducting international teleseminars that will cover everything from weight loss to relationships to setting career goals.

In 2009, Inspired Girls will produce Inspired Girls 2009 which is a young women's empowerment conference designed to uplift, inspire, and motivate young women to be their God-ordained best.

In addition to speaking at this conference, I will complete other speaking engagements throughout the year. I speak in corporate settings about the inspired workplace, goal setting and motivation. I also speak in church settings, to adults and youth alike. If you would like to learn more, you may inquire at the email address below.

Additionally, my monthly newsletter, The Inspired Life, also offers insights on a wide range of topics and how they relate to living an inspired life. If you would like to join the list or inquire about any of our products and services, please email us at info@adivinebook.com or visit us online at adivinebook.com.

WORKSHEET

Personal Inventory Worksheet

Describe yourself in 5 adjectives.
_____
_____

What is the most important thing in your life?
_____
_____

What are you passionate about?
_____
_____

What are your priorities?
_____
_____

What are the strengths of your personality?
_____
_____

Do you consider your strengths to be gifts from God?
_____
_____

What are the weaknesses of your personality?
_____
_____

What can you do to improve and eliminate your weaknesses?
_____
_____

List 5 traits that you like about yourself.
_____
_____
_____
_____
_____

List 5 traits you'd like to improve about yourself.
_____
_____
_____
_____

Where do you see yourself this time next year?
_____
_____

Where do you see yourself in 5 years?
_____
_____

Where do you see yourself in 10 years?
_____
_____

What goals would you like to achieve before you die?
_____
_____

Do you have the necessary skills/education/traits to achieve those goals?
_____
_____

If not, how can you go about getting the things you need to confidently pursue your goal?
_____
_____
_____

About the Author

Lisa Nicole Bell is a writer, entertainment professional, and entrepreneur, born and raised in Huntsville, Alabama. She graduated from California State University with a Bachelor of Science degree in Business Law. She has worked in real estate, management, and marketing. Lisa's entrepreneurial spirit and passion for helping others has resulted in the inspiration and birth of her professional creative endeavors. Lisa has invested her time in educating herself on life strategies and personal development. She has also worked in the entertainment industry in various capacities. She has starred and been featured as an actress in dozens of film and television projects. Lisa has an undying love affair with the written word and has written for magazines and publications such as LA's The Place and Positive Vibes. Lisa has also written for the stage and screen. Her most recent produced work, *Deal Breakers*, was also her directorial debut for the stage. Lisa's first book, *Divine Inspirations: Keys to Living a Divine Life*, will be published in 2009.

Lisa's company, Life With Inspiration, is a personal development and entertainment company that offers products and services with the sole aim of inspiring people. Her company achieves this goal through various mediums such as theatrical productions, printed and electronic publications, teleseminars, empowerment events and more. Lisa is steering her inspirational enterprise toward national and international success with her business savvy, interpersonal skills, and creative talent.

On a personal note, Lisa has a zest for life and makes every day count. She enjoys traveling, reading, cooking, volunteering, and painting. She enjoys spending time with her family, friends, and associates. Lisa's love for God continues to be the light on her path toward living a purposeful life and developing herself into the best woman she can be. Lisa resides in Los Angeles with her dog, Seneca.